Love Lives On
A Guide to Healing Your Heart After Pet Loss

Dr. Renee Parisi, NP

Copyright © 2025 by Renee Parisi

All rights reserved.

No part of this publication may be reproduced, distributed, or sold for commercial purposes without the express written consent of the author.
This includes—but is not limited to—photocopying, scanning, uploading, or distributing the material in print or digital formats for profit, training, or resale.

Therapists, counselors, and other licensed mental health professionals are welcome to use this book in direct patient care as part of individual or group therapy sessions, provided that:

The material is used for educational and therapeutic purposes only;

- Clients receive the material as-is, without alteration or removal of copyright notices; and
- The material is not reproduced, resold, or included in paid workshops, online courses, or other monetized programs without written permission.

To request written permission for educational, professional development, or organizational use, please contact: permissions@willowalchemy.com

This book and all accompanying materials are protected under United States copyright law.

Disclaimer

This book and its accompanying materials are intended for educational and supportive purposes only. They are not a substitute for professional medical advice, diagnosis, psychotherapy, or psychiatric care. Readers are encouraged to seek the guidance of a qualified mental health or medical professional for individualized assessment and treatment.

If you are in crisis or need immediate emotional support, please contact a local mental health helpline, your healthcare provider, or emergency services. Use of this material signifies acknowledgment and acceptance of these terms.

Table of Contents

How to Use This Book	1
1. The Bond Beyond Words Understanding Your Grief	3
Your Grief Story Activity	9
Meeting Your Pet at the Rainbow Bridge Guided Meditation	13
The Candle of Memory Ritual	19
2. The Weight of Goodbye Releasing Guilt and Finding Compassion	23
From "What If" to "Even Though" Activity	31
Forgiving Myself Guided Meditation	35
Candle of Release Ritual	39

3. The Empty Space　　　　　　　　　　　　　　　43
　　Coping With Daily Life After Loss

My Daily Rhythms of Love　　　　　　　　　　　49
Activity

Riding the Wave　　　　　　　　　　　　　　　55
Guided Meditation

Reframing Triggers as Reminders　　　　　　　　61
Activity

Creating a Comfort Corner　　　　　　　　　　67
Activity

The Daily Remembrance Practice　　　　　　　　73
Ritual

4. Paw Prints of Love　　　　　　　　　　　　　77
　　Honoring Memory & Meaning

Lessons of Love: Turning Memory Into Meaning　87
Activity

Legacy Craft Tutorial　　　　　　　　　　　　　91
Activity

Embracing Memory　　　　　　　　　　　　　97
Guided Meditation

The Legacy of Love Ceremony　　　　　　　　103
Ritual

5. Permission to Heal　　　　　　　　　　　　109
　　Reconnecting With Life

Allowing Light Back In Activity	117
Mindful Senses Activity	121
Letter From Your Pet Activity	125
Light Returning Guided Meditation	129
Moments of Softness Ritual	133
6. From Loss to Legacy Moving Forward with Grace	137
How My Love Changed Me Activity	143
Acts of Legacy Brainstorming Guide Activity	149
The Blessing Ceremony Guided Meditation	153
The Light Lives On Ritual	159
7. Chance's Legacy	163
Holding Space Journal	165

How to Use This Book

*L*ove Lives On is meant to be experienced, not just read. Inside, you'll find a blend of *reflections, activities, rituals, and guided meditations* — each designed to help you move gently through grief and reconnect with the love that remains.

Throughout the book, you'll notice spaces for writing and reflection after certain sections. These are invitations to pause, breathe, and explore your own thoughts or memories as they arise.

At the back of the print version of this book, you'll find *additional blank pages* to write, draw, paste photos, or create a memory collage of your pet. There's no right or wrong way to use them; let them become whatever you need — a journal, a keepsake, a letter, or a tribute.

Take your time. This is *your* journey — guided by love, remembrance, and gentle healing.

Chapter One

The Bond Beyond Words

Understanding Your Grief

You've arrived here because you've loved deeply—and that love deserves a space to be honored. Through this book, we'll gently walk together through the emotions, memories, and meanings of pet loss. This is not about "moving on." It's a compassionate guide to remembering with peace, releasing guilt, and rediscovering joy. Please give yourself permission to move at your own pace. You may pause, cry, journal, or simply breathe—there's no "wrong" way to grieve.

Why Pet Loss Hurts So Deeply

Losing a pet isn't "just losing an animal." It's losing a companion who offered unconditional love, safety, and comfort. When we bond with an animal, our brains release oxytocin—the same hormone that strengthens the bond between parents and children. That's why your grief feels as real and as painful as any human loss. You may notice physical sensations: heaviness in the chest, fatigue, appetite changes, or restlessness. These are normal physiological reactions to loss. Remember, your pain is proof of the love that existed.

Reflection

Pause and write a few sentences in your journal or on a page at the end of this book:

"My pet made me feel loved by…"

"When I think of them, I feel…"

The Human–Animal Bond.

Your relationship with your pet was built on a foundation of unconditional love, familiar rituals, and a companionship free from judgment. This connection wasn't "just" emotional—it was biological. Your pet activated the same attachment centers in your brain that bond parents to their children. Every cuddle, walk, and shared mealtime released soothing neurochemicals like oxytocin and dopamine, grounding your body and mind in a sense of safety and love. When that bond is broken, your heart and nervous system react as they would to any profound loss. The absence of your pet's presence can create a real sense of withdrawal—emotional, physical, and spiritual.

Why This Loss Feels Different.

Many people are caught off guard by the intensity of pet loss. Society often minimizes it, labeling it as "less than" the loss of a human, which can make your grief feel invisible or misunderstood. This is called disenfranchised grief—grief that isn't fully recognized or supported by others. You might hear things like, "It was only a pet," yet your heart knows otherwise.

Along with your beloved companion, you may have also lost daily routines like feeding, walks, or playtime; a sense of home or purpose; and the emotional anchor that made you feel safe in the world. These are real and valid losses. Grief may surface as tears, irritability, fatigue, guilt, or even numbness. There is no "right" way to grieve, only your way.

Different Forms of Pet Loss.

No two losses are the same, and each experience carries its own emotional landscape. The natural death of a pet often brings a mix of sadness and gratitude for the years shared. Euthanasia can stir complex feelings—relief, guilt, doubt, and love all existing together. A sudden accident may leave you in shock or disbelief, while a disappearance or rehoming creates ambiguous loss—a grief without closure, where the mind keeps searching for answers. Anticipatory grief, which comes with an aging or terminally ill pet, brings its own heartache as you begin saying goodbye long before the final farewell.

What Grief Does to Your Mind and Body.

Grief is not just an emotion; it's a full-body experience. You may notice changes in concentration, memory, sleep, or appetite. Your body might feel heavy, tense, or restless. You might replay moments in your mind, second-guess decisions, or feel unexpected waves of sadness in everyday moments. These reactions are not signs of weakness—they are evidence of love and of your nervous system learning how to live in a world that feels different now. Try to keep gentle routines: eat nourishing meals, rest when you can, stay hydrated, and move your body through walks, stretching, or deep breathing. When emotions feel overwhelming, reach out to trusted friends, family, or pet grief support groups.

You Are Not Alone.

Thousands of pet parents have walked this path and found light on the other side. Healing does not mean forgetting—it means remembering with peace instead of pain. As you move forward, you'll explore ways to honor your companion, process your emotions, and rebuild a sense of connection to life itself. Your love for your pet continues; it simply takes on a new form—one that lives within your heart.

Reflection

Close your eyes and picture one moment of pure joy you shared with your pet.

Breathe in that memory as light; let it fill the empty spaces with warmth.

Exhale the ache, knowing love still exists in every heartbeat that remembers.

Journal Prompt

What made my bond with my pet unique?

Which parts of daily life feel hardest right now?

What does my grief need most—rest, expression, or connection?

What Is Disenfranchised Grief?

Disenfranchised grief is the kind of mourning that goes unseen by the world. It happens when a loss is not fully acknowledged, socially validated, or publicly supported. When you lose a beloved pet, you may encounter comments like, "It was just a pet," or, "You can always get another one." While often meant to comfort, these words can pierce deeply. They fail to recognize that your bond was not replaceable—it was unique, sacred, and woven into your daily life.

Because our culture tends to reserve open mourning for human losses, many grieving pet parents feel pressured to minimize or hide their pain. This can lead to feelings of shame, confusion, or isolation, as if the depth of your sorrow must be justified or explained. Yet grief does not ask for permission—it arises naturally from love. The more your pet was part of your identity and emotional world, the more profound the loss can feel.

Here, in this space, your grief is honored. Your love is seen. You are invited to mourn as deeply and as openly as your heart needs. There is no timeline, no hierarchy of loss, and no reason to apologize for your tears. Grieving a beloved animal is an act of love, not weakness—it is proof of the bond that transformed your life.

Journal Prompt

Write about a time someone dismissed or misunderstood your grief.

How did their response make you feel?

What words, if any, would have comforted you instead?

Affirmation

"My grief is valid. My love deserves space."

Your Grief Story

Activity

This activity helps you honor the story of your beloved companion—the moments you shared, the lessons they taught you, and the love that will always remain. There are no right or wrong answers. Allow your heart to lead the way.

About My Pet

Pet's Name:

- Nicknames or special names I used:

- Species/Breed:

- Age at passing:

- Date of Birth (or Gotcha Day):

- Date of Passing:

Our First Chapter

How did your pet come into your life? Describe the first day you met them and how you felt.

The Bond We Shared

What made your relationship special?

What were your favorite routines, habits, or quirks that made you smile?

My Pet's Personality

If your pet could talk, what would they say about life?

How would you describe their spirit or energy?

A Favorite Memory

Write about one memory that brings you the most joy or peace when you think about your pet.

What My Pet Taught Me

What lessons did your pet teach you about love, patience, or life?

The Hardest Goodbye

Describe the moment you realized you would have to say goodbye. What helped you get through that time—or what would have helped?

Continuing the Connection

In what ways do you still feel connected to your pet today?

Are there signs, memories, or sensations that remind you of them?

A Message TO My Pet

Write a short message to your pet—something you wish you could tell them right now.

A Message FROM My Pet

If your pet could send you a message from beyond, what do you think they would say?

Reflection

"The love between a human and an animal does not end with death. It simply changes form— from physical presence to eternal connection."

Take a moment to breathe and honor the story you've just told. This story—your pet's story—is part of your healing journey.

Meeting Your Pet at the Rainbow Bridge

Guided Meditation

For grief healing and heart connection after the loss of a beloved animal companion. Before we begin, find a quiet, comfortable space where you can relax without interruption. You may wish to have a photo of your pet nearby, or an item that reminds you of them—a collar, a toy, or a small keepsake.

Take a moment to close your eyes.

Allow your body to settle into stillness.

Let your hands rest gently on your heart, and feel the soft rhythm of your breath moving in and out.

With every inhale, you breathe in calm.

With every exhale, you release tension, grief, and heaviness.

Let the world outside fade away as you enter a place of stillness, peace, and remembrance.

Grounding the Heart

Take a deep breath in through your nose…

and exhale slowly through your mouth.

Imagine a soft, golden light surrounding your heart.

This light represents love—the same love that always connected you and your pet.

With every breath, this light grows brighter and warmer.

It expands through your chest, your shoulders, your arms, and down into your hands.

You are surrounded now by the energy of love, warmth, and safety.

This light becomes a bridge—a pathway that connects your heart to theirs.

The Journey Begins

Now, imagine you are standing in a serene meadow at the edge of a forest.

The air is fresh, scented with wildflowers and soft rain.

You can hear a gentle stream flowing nearby and birds singing overhead.

In the distance, you see a magnificent rainbow arching across the sky—vivid, luminous, and alive.

This is the Rainbow Bridge—a sacred place where souls reunite.

A place of unconditional love where no pain or illness exists.

As you begin walking toward the rainbow, notice how light and peaceful your steps feel.

Each footstep releases another layer of grief and brings you closer to love.

The Reunion

At the foot of the rainbow, you see a figure approaching.

At first, it's only a shimmer of light...

but soon, that light takes shape.

Their outline becomes familiar—the curve of their ears, the way they move, the glimmer in their eyes.

It's them.

Your beloved pet.

Notice their joy as they recognize you.

Their tail wags, or they purr softly, or they bound toward you just as they always did.

You kneel, and they come running into your arms.

You can feel their warmth, their heartbeat, their fur, their breath.

Take a moment here to simply be together.

Let yourself feel their presence—pure, alive, radiant with love.

Heart-to-Heart Connection

Now, imagine a golden thread of light connecting your heart to theirs.

This is the eternal bond that never breaks.

Even though they are on a different plane, this love flows freely between you—unlimited by time or distance.

If there are words you wish to say to them, whisper them now.

You might say thank you…

You might say I miss you…

You might simply say, I love you.

Listen now—perhaps you sense a response.

Maybe it's a feeling, a word, or a knowing deep in your heart.

Let their message wash over you with peace and comfort.

Crossing the Bridge Together

Your pet turns toward the rainbow and begins to walk with you.

The light around you both becomes softer, shimmering with every color.

You walk together for a few moments more—no pain, no fear, only love.

When you reach the center of the bridge, your pet pauses and looks back at you.

Their eyes tell you everything you need to know:

They are safe.

They are free.

And they will always be with you—just on the other side of the rainbow.

They nuzzle your hand one last time, then walk forward into the light.

The rainbow glows even brighter as they disappear into the horizon of peace.

Returning Home with Love

You stand for a moment, bathed in warmth and gratitude.

You know that the love you share can never be lost.

It lives on—within your memories, your heart, and the gentle signs they send.

Now take a deep breath in, drawing that peace into your chest.

Exhale, releasing any remaining sorrow.

Slowly, allow the image of the rainbow to fade.

Feel yourself returning to the present moment—grounded, calm, and comforted.

When you are ready, open your eyes.

You have met your beloved pet again—heart-to-heart, soul to soul.

And they remain with you, always.

Affirmation

"Love is not bound by life or death. It flows endlessly between our souls, until we meet again at the Rainbow Bridge."

The Candle of Memory

Ritual

Lighting a candle is one of the oldest ways to honor a life that has passed. This ritual invites you to pause, breathe, and reconnect with your pet's love in a space of quiet remembrance. Each time you light your candle, you create a bridge between memory and presence—reminding your heart that love continues to exist, just in a different form.

What You'll Need

A candle that feels special to you. Choose a color or scent that reminds you of your pet.

(Examples: soft white for peace, blue for comfort, gold for joy, green for renewal.)

A small photo, collar tag, or keepsake.

A safe space—a quiet area free of distractions where you can sit comfortably.

A journal or notepad (optional) to write thoughts that come up.

Music: Play a song that reminds you of peaceful time together.

Scent: Add a drop of lavender or sandalwood oil nearby for grounding.

Repeat: This ritual can be done weekly—on birthdays, adoption anniversaries, or any day you miss them most.

Prepare the Space

Find a quiet corner and place your candle in front of you.

Arrange your keepsake nearby.

Take three slow breaths—each exhale releasing the weight of the day.

Set the Intention

Whisper or think softly: "This light is for you, my beloved friend. May it shine where your spirit runs free."

Light the Candle

As the flame flickers, imagine it carrying your love upward, connecting earth and spirit.

Watch how the light moves—it's okay if tears come. Let them. They are a language of love.

Remember

Say your pet's name aloud.

Recall one moment that makes you smile—a silly habit, a favorite walk, the sound of their paws.

You may speak it aloud, write it down, or simply feel it.

Close the Ritual

Before extinguishing the candle, say: "Your light lives on in me. Thank you for every moment."

Gently blow out the flame, visualizing the light continuing inside your heart.

Reflection

After the ritual, write or think about:

What memory surfaced most vividly?

What emotion felt strongest—love, sadness, gratitude, peace?

How did your body feel before and after the candle was lit?

Each candle you light is a promise to remember, not with pain, but with presence.

Grief transforms, but love remains unchanged—it continues to glow through every act of remembrance.

Affirmation

"My grief honors the depth of my love."

End-of-Chapter Check-In:

1. Do I better understand why my grief feels so strong?

2. Have I given myself permission to feel without judgment?

3. What memory of my pet brings me warmth instead of pain?

Chapter Two

The Weight of Goodbye

Releasing Guilt and Finding Compassion

Welcome back, friend.

In this chapter, we'll explore one of the most tender parts of grief — the goodbye. Whether you've already said goodbye or are preparing for that moment, you may feel waves of guilt, regret, or uncertainty. I want you to remember: you acted from love. You made the best decision you could with the information and care you had. Now is time to release blame and learn to hold your heart gently as you heal.

Understanding Guilt and Grief After Pet Loss

When we lose a beloved animal, guilt often becomes one of the loudest emotions. We may replay our choices—Did I do enough? Should I have noticed sooner? Could I have waited longer before saying goodbye? Psychologically, guilt gives us the illusion of control. The mind tries to find meaning in something that feels senseless by searching for what could have been changed. It's our brain's way of saying, "If I can find the mistake, maybe I can undo the pain." But guilt doesn't heal—it keeps us trapped in "what-ifs."

The Truth About Loving and Losing

Love always carries risk. When you open your heart to another being—human or animal—you also open yourself to the ache of loss. Yet that same vulnerability is what makes love profound. Every decision you made for your pet was rooted in love, care, and the information you had at the time. Self-compassion means recognizing that you were doing your best, even when outcomes were beyond your control.

How Guilt Manifests

Responsibility Guilt: "I should have done more."

Survivor's Guilt: "Why did I live when they didn't?"

Relief Guilt: "Why do I feel a little lighter now that the suffering is over?"

All of these are normal reactions. None mean you loved your pet any less.

Transforming Guilt Through Compassion

Name the Emotion: Say aloud, "This is guilt." Naming it helps separate you from it.

Acknowledge Intention: Remember what guided your choices—love, care, mercy, protection.

Speak Kindly to Yourself: Ask, "What would I say to a friend feeling this way?" Then offer those same words to yourself.

Reframe the Story: Instead of "I failed," say "I loved deeply and made the best choices I could."

Allow Grace: Healing does not mean forgetting. It means allowing love to exist beside sorrow.

Reflection

"Grief is love that has nowhere to go."

When guilt arises, gently remind yourself: My love was real. My actions were rooted in care. My pet knew they were safe and loved.

Practice a Compassion Pause

Take a slow breath.

Place a hand over your heart.

Whisper:

"I did my best.

My best was enough.

Love remains."

Self-compassion doesn't erase grief—it softens its edges. It allows healing to unfold naturally, replacing guilt with gratitude, and pain with quiet remembrance. Be gentle with yourself. The love you gave—and continue to feel—is the clearest proof of a bond that endures beyond life itself.

The Compassionate Choice: Understanding Euthanasia and Guilt

Euthanasia can be one of the hardest words to even say — and one of the most compassionate acts we can give. Our pets trust us completely. When illness or suffering becomes too great, the most loving gift we can offer is peace. Yet, our human hearts often confuse compassion with guilt. Remember: choosing mercy over prolonging suffering is not a betrayal — it's love in its most selfless form. Guilt is a sign of love, not wrongdoing.

The Psychology of Anticipatory Grief, Cognitive Dissonance, and the Emotional Aftermath

Choosing euthanasia for a beloved pet is one of the most painful—and profoundly selfless—decisions a person can face. It requires holding two opposing truths at once: the desire to end your pet's suffering, and the desperate wish not to say goodbye. This inner conflict—love versus loss, protection versus pain—creates an emotional tension that few other experiences can match. The act is often called compassionate euthanasia because it arises not from giving up, but from giving peace. It is an expression of love in its purest form: love that releases, even when every part of you wants to hold on.

Cognitive Dissonance: The Inner Conflict

Cognitive dissonance occurs when two conflicting beliefs or emotions exist at the same time. When deciding on euthanasia, this may sound like: "I know it's the kindest choice, but it feels like betrayal." Or "I want them free from pain, but I still want more time." You may tell yourself, "I'm doing what's best," yet feel a deep sense of failure. This tug-of-war in the mind is not weakness—it is the natural result of trying to make sense of an impossible situation. Both sides of the conflict are true: you can love your pet deeply and still grieve the decision profoundly. You can feel both peace and pain in the same breath. Accepting that paradox allows compassion to return—to your pet, and to yourself.

The Emotional Aftermath

After euthanasia, emotions rarely follow a straight line. Relief that your pet's suffering has ended can be quickly followed by guilt for feeling relief at all. You might second-guess the timing, wonder if there was something else you could have tried, or replay the final moments in your mind—wishing you had held them longer or said something differently. Numbness and disbelief often mix with deep sadness and emptiness. These conflicting emotions are not proof that you made the wrong choice; they are evidence of how much you loved, and how deeply you cared. The very struggle you feel is love trying to find a new shape in a world that no longer includes your pet's physical presence.

How to Begin Healing

Healing begins by naming what is true. Acknowledge the complexity of your emotions—relief, guilt, gratitude, sadness. They can coexist. Forgive yourself for being human. You acted from love and courage, and while the outcome was loss, the intention was mercy. Create small rituals to honor your companion's life: light a candle, plant a flower, frame a favorite photo, or write a farewell letter. Rituals give structure to sorrow, transforming pain into remembrance. Seek support from people who understand—whether through counseling, pet loss groups, or compassionate friends. And most importantly, allow yourself to rest. Emotional exhaustion is a natural part of grief; gentleness toward yourself is not indulgence, it is healing.

When the pain of suffering outweighs the joy of living, love sometimes asks us to let go. Compassionate euthanasia is not an act of abandonment—it is an act of devotion. Your pet's peace is the legacy of your love, a final gift born from the same care that guided every moment of your life together.

Exercise

Write a letter titled "What Love Looked Like That Day."

Describe what you did for your pet — the comfort you offered, the care you showed, and the love that surrounded them.

Anticipatory Grief: The Goodbye That Begins Before the End

Sometimes, grief begins long before the final goodbye. It starts quietly—the moment you notice your pet's slowing steps, their changing appetite, or the gentle cloudiness in their eyes. It may come with a vet's diagnosis or a growing awareness that time together is becoming precious and limited. This early form of mourning is called anticipatory grief. It is the heart and body's way of preparing for what lies ahead—a natural, protective process that allows us to begin saying goodbye even as we continue to hold on.

Anticipatory grief often brings a confusing mix of emotions. One day may feel full of gratitude and peace, and the next may be shadowed by dread or guilt. You might find yourself hoping for a miracle while also trying to accept reality. Moments of laughter or relief can quickly turn into tears, and that emotional whiplash can feel disorienting. Yet these swings are not signs of instability; they are the language of love adjusting to change. You are not "giving up" when you recognize that the end is approaching—you are learning how to hold both love and loss at once.

During this time, it's important to allow yourself to feel it all. Cherish the small rituals—shared meals, quiet naps, the familiar sound of paws on the floor. Take photos, speak tender words, and create memories that will become a source of comfort later. Acknowledge the sadness that comes with each change, but also the deep gratitude that you still have moments to give and receive love. This dual awareness—honoring both what remains and what is ending—is not disloyal. It is love, adapting to what is.

Letting Go of the "What Ifs"

One of the most common emotions after losing a beloved pet is guilt. It often takes the shape of endless "what if" questions—What if I had noticed the signs sooner? What if I'd chosen a different treatment? What if I had done more? These thoughts can loop endlessly, as the mind tries to rewrite the past in an effort to undo the pain of loss. This is a natural human response. When something we love deeply ends, our brain searches for a sense of control—believing that if we had just acted differently, the outcome might have changed. But grief is not a problem to be solved. It is an experience that must be lived through, felt fully, and met with compassion.

Healing begins when we shift from "what if" to "even though." This gentle reframe allows space for both sorrow and self-forgiveness. Instead of chasing impossible alternate versions of the past, we begin to honor the truth of what we did give:

care, comfort, and love. Saying, "Even though I wish I'd had more time, I know my love was enough," opens the heart to acceptance. It acknowledges the pain without being consumed by it.

Try practicing the "Even Though" Reframing Technique. Write down a few statements that help you release guilt and embrace grace. For example:

Even though I wish I could have done more, I know I did my best.

Even though it hurts, I gave my pet peace and dignity.

Even though I feel guilty, I acted from love.

Each "even though" statement creates a bridge between heartbreak and healing. It reminds you that love, not perfection, defined your bond—and that love is what endures.

Reflection

What has anticipatory grief looked like for me?

What do I want to remember about this time?

Affirmation:

"I honor both love and loss in the same breath."

From "What If" to "Even Though"

Activity

After the loss of a beloved pet, it's common to replay moments and decisions—asking "What if I had noticed sooner?" or "What if I had chosen differently?" These thoughts are part of the mind's attempt to regain control after something that felt uncontrollable. But the truth is: love and loss coexist, and hindsight is always clearer than the moment itself. This activity helps you gently move from self-criticism to self-compassion, one thought at a time.

Step 1: Identify the "What If" Thought

Write down one or more thoughts that replay in your mind.

(Examples: "What if I had taken her to the vet earlier?" "What if I hadn't agreed to euthanasia?")

My 'What If' Thought:

Step 2: Explore the Feelings Behind It

What emotion is underneath the "what if"? Guilt, regret, sadness, helplessness, love?

What is this emotion trying to tell you?

Step 3: Acknowledge What You Could and Couldn't Control

Turn to a blank page at the back of this book. Make two columns. In the columns make a list of what was within your control and what was not at the time. (Be honest and gentle with yourself.)

Step 4: Shift to "Even Though"

Reframe your thought using the words **"Even though..."** to create space for compassion and truth.

Examples:

What if I waited too long? → **Even though I wish I could have acted sooner, I made every choice out of love and care.**

What if I failed him? → **Even though I couldn't save him, I gave him comfort, safety, and unconditional love..**

What if I was wrong? → **Even though I'll never have all the answers, my heart guided me with the best knowledge I had.**

Step 5: Anchor the Reframe in Compassion

Complete the sentence below as a way to ground yourself in gentleness:

"Even though I feel _____, I know that I _____."

(Example: "Even though I feel guilty, I know that I loved deeply.")

Step 6: Reflection

What shifted as you wrote your "even though" statement?

How does your body feel now compared to when you began?

What would you say to a friend who felt the same way?

Forgiving Myself

Guided Meditation

Find a quiet, comfortable space where you can sit or lie down without interruption.

You may wish to hold a photo of your pet or place your hand over your heart.

Take your time — this meditation is meant to be felt, not rushed.

Settle the Body

Take a slow breath in through your nose...

and exhale softly through your mouth.

Let your shoulders relax, your jaw unclench, and your thoughts begin to slow.

Remind yourself:

"Right now, I am safe. I am here."

Invite the Light of Forgiveness

Imagine a soft golden light resting over your heart.

It glows gently — warm, steady, kind.

This light is forgiveness.

It carries no blame, no judgment — only understanding.

With each inhale, the light grows stronger.

With each exhale, it melts away tension and guilt.

Let it spread through your chest and down your arms,

soothing every part of you that's been holding pain.

See Your Pet in the Light

Now picture your pet standing within that same golden glow.

They are healthy, joyful, and free.

Their eyes sparkle with recognition and love.

See them looking up at you as if to say:

"Thank you for loving me.

Thank you for giving me peace.

Thank you for being my home."

Breathe in that love.

Let it soften the ache in your heart.

Release the Weight

With every breath, imagine the heaviness of guilt loosening.

Each exhale carries it away like a soft gray mist fading into the sky.

Tears may come — let them. They are part of the release.

As the mist clears, notice what remains: warmth, gratitude, peace.

The light grows brighter now, wrapping you in compassion —

the same unconditional love your pet always offered you.

Repeat the Words of Forgiveness

Whisper softly or repeat in your mind:

"I forgive myself.

I acted from love.

I release the rest."

Say it again, slower:

"I forgive myself.

I acted from love.

I release the rest."

Let these words echo gently through your body.

Feel the truth of them sink deeper with every breath.

Return to Peace

Take one final deep breath in...

and exhale completely.

Notice how your heart feels now — warm, open, lighter than before.

The golden light remains within you, steady and calm.

Your pet's love shines there too.

You are forgiven.

You are loved.

You are healing.

Affirmation

"I forgive myself. My love was enough. My heart is healing. Peace lives within me."

Reflection

After completing this meditation, take a few minutes to journal:

What emotions surfaced as you imagined your pet in the light?

What does "acting from love" mean to you in this context?

How can you remind yourself of forgiveness when guilt resurfaces?

Candle of Release

Ritual

This ritual is designed to help you gently release guilt, regret, and self-blame — emotions that often linger after the loss of a beloved animal companion. It honors both your love and your humanity, recognizing that you did the best you could with what you knew at the time.

Prepare Your Space:

Choose a quiet, comfortable place where you won't be interrupted. Dim the lights, silence your phone, and allow yourself to be fully present.

You may wish to place a photo of your pet nearby, or hold a small object that reminds you of them — a collar, toy, or keepsake.

Set Your Intention:

As you light your candle, imagine the flame as a symbol of love — the bond that continues between you and your pet. Feel the warmth of that light expanding in your chest, softening the heavy places inside you.

Speak Aloud or Silently Within:

"I did my best.

I gave love freely and fully.

I release the guilt that no longer serves me.

I forgive myself for being human.

I trust that my pet knew my love — then and now."

Allow the words to settle into your heart. You may repeat them several times, or add your own words of release and forgiveness.

Breathe and Let Go:

With each slow exhale, imagine releasing one small piece of guilt, regret, or doubt — as if it were smoke rising from the candle and disappearing into the air. You don't need to let it all go at once. Even releasing a single thread of guilt is a sacred act of healing.

Close the Ritual:

When you feel ready, take a final deep breath. Whisper a quiet thank you — to your pet, to yourself, and to the love you shared.

Then, blow out the candle slowly, watching the smoke curl and fade — a symbol of peace returning to your heart.

Sit in the stillness that follows. You may wish to write down how you feel or what you've released in a journal or in the back of this book.

Reflection

What guilt or regret did I release today?

What truth or comfort rose in its place?

Affirmation

"I release guilt and hold onto love. My heart is learning to rest."

End-of-Chapter Check-In:

1. Have I recognized guilt as a form of love, not failure?

2. Can I speak to myself with compassion instead of judgment?

3. What truth about my pet's passing brings me a small measure of peace?

Chapter Three

The Empty Space

Coping With Daily Life After Loss

Welcome back, friend.

By now, you've faced the hardest parts of goodbye and begun to release guilt. In this chapter, we step into the stillness that follows. The quiet moments — the empty bowls, the leash on the hook, the missing footsteps — can feel heavy. But this emptiness isn't a punishment. It's love's echo. Together, we'll learn how to live with that echo — to turn absence into gentle presence.

The Silence After Goodbye

After the loss of a beloved pet, it is often the quiet moments that ache the most—the stillness of morning when no one is waiting to be fed, the empty spot on the couch, the silence where familiar sounds used to live. This "empty space" is not only physical; it is deeply emotional and neurological. It reflects the bond your body and mind built through countless small acts of care, comfort, and connection. Your pet became part of your daily rhythm, part of the sensory world that told your nervous system: I am safe, I am loved, I am home. When that presence is gone, it is natural for your entire being to feel the void.

Grief and the Rhythm of Routine

Our pets give structure to our days. Their needs create purpose, and their joy brings balance. Feeding them, walking them, greeting them after work—these predictable moments train the brain to anticipate love and connection. When those routines suddenly disappear, the nervous system feels it as loss, confusion, and disorientation. That's because routines are regulatory—they help keep the body's stress and comfort systems in harmony. The act of caring for your pet regularly released oxytocin, the bonding hormone, while lowering cortisol, the stress hormone. These chemical patterns signaled your body that you were safe. When the routine vanishes, your nervous system goes into alert mode, sensing danger in the unfamiliar quiet. The result can feel like anxiety, restlessness, or emotional numbness.

Why You May Feel "Off"

In the days and weeks following loss, you may feel unlike yourself. Restlessness, trouble sleeping, loss of appetite, or eating at odd hours are common. You might feel jumpy, unfocused, or notice sudden waves of panic or tightness in your chest. Many describe a strange sense of emptiness or "not knowing what to do" with themselves. These are not weaknesses or failures—they are the body's way of recalibrating to life without the cues it once relied on for emotional safety. Your nervous system is learning a new rhythm, one that takes time to develop.

Ways to Support Your Nervous System

Healing begins with gentle new signals of safety and stability. You can start small.

Maintain a morning ritual, even if your mornings once revolved around your pet. Light a candle, open a window, or whisper their name in gratitude. Keeping a familiar rhythm tells your body the world still holds order.

Move your body, even briefly—walk at the same time you used to walk your pet, or stretch softly to release stored tension. Movement communicates safety and helps the body process grief.

Ground through your senses. Notice textures, scents, and sounds around you: the softness of a blanket, the warmth of a mug, sunlight on your face. These sensory anchors soothe the vagus nerve, calming your system.

Speak your pet's name aloud in conversation, prayer, or reflection. Doing so reassures both your mind and body that love and connection still exist, even if in a new form.

And above all, create predictability again. Grief thrives in chaos, but healing thrives in rhythm. Choose one simple activity—journaling, meditation, or a daily walk—and let it become your new anchor in the day.

The Psychology of the Empty Space

It's common to feel uncertain about your identity after loss. When daily care routines vanish, the mind struggles to reconcile the absence of purpose. You may wonder who you are without your caregiving role, or what to do with your time and love now that your pet is gone. This is not regression—it is reorganization. Your brain and heart are learning to exist without the constant sensory feedback your pet once provided. Over time, this empty space doesn't close—it transforms. It becomes a sacred place where love lives on, not by replacing your pet, but by carrying their memory forward in meaningful new ways.

Why Silence Feels So Loud: The Neuroscience of Habit and Loss

Our brains are beautifully, and sometimes painfully, wired for repetition. Every time you fed your pet, clipped on the leash, or settled in together at night, your brain recorded those moments as predictable patterns of comfort. Over time, these routines became part of your neural rhythm—a steady beat of love and safety that structured your days. When those routines suddenly vanish, the brain doesn't immediately understand that the pattern has changed. It still expects the sound of paws on the floor, the rustle of food bags, or the weight of your pet beside you. When the brain reaches for those cues and finds only silence, it triggers a sense of disorientation, longing, or deep sadness. This is why ordinary moments—walking into a quiet room, hearing a jingle that sounds like a collar, or glancing toward an empty spot—can unexpectedly bring you to tears.

This reaction isn't a sign that something is wrong with you; it's evidence of how deeply your pet became part of your nervous system's daily rhythm. Grief interrupts those familiar neural pathways, leaving your body and mind searching for what once brought regulation and peace. Understanding this helps transform frustration or self-blame into compassion. You're not "stuck in grief" or "overreacting"—you're a human being whose brain is trying to adapt to a world missing one of its most soothing signals.

To begin rebalancing those rhythms, try a simple reflection exercise. Write down three daily routines that once centered on your pet—perhaps morning feedings, evening walks, or bedtime cuddles. Then, circle one you'd like to transform into a healing ritual rather than an absence. If you used to take evening walks together, you might continue walking at the same time, dedicating those steps to your pet's memory. If you shared morning quiet moments, you could light a candle or speak a word of gratitude in their honor. These gentle acts help your brain create new associations—transforming the ache of silence into moments of meaning, and helping your heart learn a new rhythm of remembrance and peace.

Reflection

The body remembers touch. The heart remembers presence. The soul remembers love. The emptiness you feel now is not absence—it is the echo of a bond that shaped your nervous system, your days, and your heart. With patience, tenderness, and time, that space softens. The ache begins to breathe again. What once felt like emptiness slowly becomes peace—a living testament to the love that remains.

Journal Prompt

"What part of my day feels the emptiest since my pet's passing? What emotion shows up most strongly during that time?"

My Daily Rhythms of Love

Activity

When we share our lives with an animal, love is expressed through routine—feeding, walking, cuddling, or simply being together. After loss, those daily acts of care disappear, leaving the nervous system searching for the rhythm it once relied on. This worksheet helps you gently honor your old routines while creating new ones that continue the love in a different form.

Step 1: Remember the Rhythm

Think about the moments in your day that once included your pet.

Time of Day | What We Did Together | How It Made Me Feel

Morning

Afternoon

Evening

Bedtime

Which part of your day feels the emptiest now?

Step 2: Acknowledge the Emotion

When those quiet moments come, what emotions do you notice most?

☐ Sadness

☐ Loneliness

☐ Guilt

☐ Restlessness

☐ Peace

☐ Gratitude

☐ Other:

What does your body feel like during those times (heavy, tight, tired, jittery, calm)?

Step 3: Honor the Old Routine

Write a short message of thanks to your pet for the daily rhythm you shared.

Example: "Thank you for our morning walks and for greeting me every day. You made ordinary moments sacred."

Step 4: Rebuild a New Rhythm

Now, choose one or two times of day when you'll create a new ritual that honors the love you shared.

Time of Day | New Ritual or Practice | How It Supports Me

Morning

Afternoon

Evening

Bedtime

Examples:

- Light a candle at the time I used to feed my pet
- Take a short walk and whisper a memory
- Journal for 5 minutes in the evening
- Hold their photo and breathe deeply

Step 5: Anchor in the Present Moment

"Love once expressed in care can now be expressed in stillness."

When you feel the ache of an empty moment, pause and ask yourself:

1. What part of my day am I missing?

2. What can I do right now to bring warmth, rhythm, or presence into this moment?

Step 6: A Closing Affirmation

Complete this statement:

"Even though my days feel different now, they are still filled with love because…"

Gentle Reminder

Healing is not about filling the empty space—it's about allowing new meaning to grow inside it.

Your pet's rhythm of love continues through the way you care for yourself today.

***

When the Wave Hits: Managing Emotional Triggers

Grief often arrives in waves. A sound, a smell, or an empty spot can pull you under. But waves are temporary — they rise, crest, and fall.

The goal isn't to stop the waves; it's to learn to float.

Exercise: Grounding Technique

1. Pause and name the trigger. ("This is grief.")

2. Breathe: In for 4 counts, out for 6.

3. Place a hand over your heart.

4. Repeat: "This feeling is love remembering."

5. Return to the present: Notice one color, one sound, one texture around you.

Reflection Prompt:

"What helps me stay afloat when the wave of grief rises?"

Riding the Wave
Guided Meditation

Find a quiet, comfortable space where you can sit or lie down.

If it feels right, place a hand over your heart or rest your palms on your thighs.

Take a slow breath in through your nose... and exhale softly through your mouth.

Allow your body to begin softening.

This meditation is here to help you ride the wave of emotion — not fight it, not fear it — but let it pass through gently.

Naming the Wave

Close your eyes.

Bring your attention inward and notice what you feel right now.

Is there tightness in your chest?

A heaviness in your stomach?

Perhaps your throat feels full, or your eyes begin to sting with tears.

Whatever you find, name it softly in your mind.

"This is grief."

"This is love missing its home."

There's no need to push it away.

Simply recognize it and breathe.

Naming what you feel brings steadiness — it reminds your body that emotion is safe to experience.

Finding Your Anchor

Now bring awareness to the parts of your body that feel supported.

Feel your feet on the floor, your back against the chair, or the surface beneath you.

Imagine soft roots extending from the soles of your feet down into the earth.

With every exhale, those roots grow deeper.

With every inhale, you draw strength from the ground below you.

You are anchored.

You are safe.

Even as the waves rise, you remain connected to something steady and unmovable beneath you.

Breathing Through the Wave

Shift your focus to your breath.

Inhale slowly through your nose for a count of four...

Pause for a moment...

Then exhale through your mouth for a count of six.

Feel your chest rise and fall like the ocean's surface.

The wave comes — you rise with it.

The wave falls — you drift back down.

You don't need to control it.

You only need to breathe and move with it.

Repeat silently to yourself:

"I can feel this and stay safe."

"The wave will pass."

Allowing the Emotion to Move

Notice where the emotion lives in your body.

Perhaps it feels like pressure in your chest or a vibration in your throat.

Instead of resisting it, imagine creating space around it with your breath.

With every inhale, you expand your capacity to hold what you feel.

With every exhale, you release what's too heavy to carry right now.

Picture the wave moving through you — energy in motion, not something to fight.

You are not the wave.

You are the ocean — vast, deep, capable of holding it all.

Returning to Shore

Now imagine the waters beginning to calm.

The wave that once felt so strong is softening, settling, fading into stillness.

You are floating gently, supported by the surface of the ocean, breathing with ease.

As you return to shore, feel your body grounded again.

Notice the sensation of the floor beneath you, the temperature of the air, the rhythm of your heartbeat.

Whisper quietly to yourself:

"I survived this wave."

"I am learning to flow with my grief."

"Peace returns to me, one breath at a time."

Closing the Practice

Take one last deep breath in through your nose...

and exhale slowly through your mouth.

Place your hand over your heart.

Feel your heartbeat — steady and sure.

This rhythm is your anchor; it reminds you that you are alive, healing, and whole.

When you're ready, open your eyes.

You are grounded.

You are calm.

You are safe.

Affirmation

"Grief is a wave, but I am the ocean, I rise, I fall, I return to calm. Love is the current that carries me home."

Reflection

After completing this meditation, you may wish to write or reflect on:

What sensations or emotions arose during the wave?

What helped you feel anchored or safe?

What can you remind yourself the next time a wave of grief begins to rise?

Reframing Triggers as Reminders

Activity

After losing a beloved pet, even the smallest things can unexpectedly bring a wave of emotion—the sound of keys by the door, the sight of a leash, or a particular spot on the couch. These triggers can feel cruel at first, as if they reopen the wound just when you thought it was starting to heal. But in truth, triggers are proof that love once filled that space. Each one is a small doorway back to connection—a moment where memory, love, and loss meet in the same heartbeat.

When you reframe a trigger from "painful reminder" to "love remembered," you begin to take your power back from grief. Instead of fearing the moments that make your chest tighten, you can meet them with gentle acknowledgment. A trigger doesn't have to mean suffering—it can become an invitation to pause and feel gratitude for what you shared. This shift doesn't erase the ache, but it allows beauty to coexist with sorrow.

Try this exercise to practice reframing. Write down three common triggers that have surfaced since your loss—perhaps the sound of keys jingling, an empty food bowl, or the sight of your pet's favorite toy. Next to each one, write a loving memory connected to it. For example: "His leash → our sunset walks." Then, at the end of each line, add the phrase, "Thank you for reminding me."

This simple act transforms the moment from one of pain into one of presence. Instead of avoiding reminders, you begin to greet them as gentle echoes of love—a sign that your bond still lives on in memory, in emotion, and in the quiet corners of your heart.

Feeling triggered doesn't mean you're "going backward" in your healing—it means your love and memory are still very much alive. This activity will help you recognize those moments, understand what they're teaching you, and find gentler ways to respond.

Step 1: Identify Your Triggers

Think of moments that have recently brought up waves of emotion.

Write them below or use one of the pages in the back of this book.

Trigger (What Happened) → Emotion(s) → Felt Intensity (1-10)

Emotion(s):

Felt Intensity (1–10):

Example: Hearing the jingling of a leash → Sadness, tears → 8/10

Step 2: Understand the Meaning Behind the Emotion

Each trigger is connected to a memory or unmet need.

Ask yourself:

What does this remind me of?

What part of my relationship with my pet does this touch?

What does my body need right now—comfort, rest, reassurance?

Write your reflections here:

Step 3: Reframe the Trigger

Reframing doesn't mean ignoring pain—it means giving it new meaning.

Use the sentence below to help transform each trigger into an expression of continuing love.

Trigger → Old Thought → New Reframe ("Even though... / This means...")

Examples:

- Old Thought: "I can't look at their toys—it hurts too much."

 New Reframe: "Even though it hurts, it reminds me how much joy we shared."

- Old Thought: "Seeing other dogs makes me angry."

 New Reframe: "This reminds me how special my bond was, and that love like that is rare."

Step 4: Create a Grounding Plan

When a trigger appears, the goal isn't to suppress it—but to stay present with compassion.

Choose one or two grounding strategies that feel right for you:

☐ Deep breathing (inhale 4, hold 4, exhale 6)

☐ Touch something comforting (a blanket, a photo, your pet's collar)

☐ Repeat a calming affirmation

☐ Step outside for fresh air

☐ Light a candle and take three mindful breaths

☐ Other:

My personal grounding phrase or action:

Step 5: Reaffirm Love and Progress

"This wave of emotion is a sign of how deeply I loved.

It doesn't erase my healing—it reminds me of connection."

Write one positive truth to carry with you when triggers appear:

Reflection

Triggers may feel like setbacks, but they are really moments of remembering.

Each wave of emotion is the nervous system learning how to hold love and loss in the same space.

With time, the sharpness softens—and what remains is gratitude.

Creating a Comfort Corner

Activity

After the loss of a beloved pet, it can be grounding to create a small, intentional space where love still feels tangible. This is sometimes called a comfort corner—a place where memory and presence meet. It doesn't need to be elaborate or large; it might be a shelf, a bedside table, or a sunny windowsill. In this space, you can place a few items that hold meaning: a framed photo, your pet's collar or favorite toy, a candle, or a small crystal or flower that symbolizes peace. Each object serves as a quiet touchstone, helping your heart reconnect to feelings of love instead of absence.

Think of this not as a shrine of sadness, but as a sanctuary of love. It's a space that honors your bond and gives you permission to pause, breathe, and remember. Sitting here for a few moments each day can calm the nervous system, offering both comfort and continuity. It can be a place to cry, to reflect, or simply to feel close to your pet's spirit when the world feels overwhelming.

You might choose to light a candle and whisper your pet's name, journal nearby, or rest your hand on one of their belongings while taking deep breaths. There's no right or wrong way to use this space—only what brings you peace. Over time, the comfort corner becomes a symbol of enduring connection, reminding you that love doesn't end with loss; it simply changes form.

Comfort Corner Checklist: Creating a Safe and Soothing Space for Healing

Step 1: Choose Your Space

☐ Quiet corner of a room

☐ A favorite chair or reading nook

☐ Outdoor garden spot

☐ Beside your pet's photo or memorial stone

☐ Other meaningful place:

Where I'll create my Comfort Corner:

Step 2: Gather Meaningful Objects

Select items that bring peace, memory, and grounding.

Use this checklist as inspiration—there's no right or wrong way to create your space.

Memory Items

- ☐ Photo of your pet
- ☐ Their collar or tag
- ☐ A paw print or fur clipping
- ☐ Favorite toy or blanket
- ☐ Candle or LED light
- ☐ Framed quote or poem
- ☐ A letter you've written to your pet

Soothing Sensory Objects

- ☐ Soft blanket or pillow
- ☐ Essential oils (lavender, chamomile, sandalwood)
- ☐ A smooth stone or crystal (rose quartz for love, amethyst for peace)
- ☐ A warm mug or calming tea
- ☐ Gentle music or nature sounds
- ☐ Weighted lap blanket or stuffed animal

Spiritual or Symbolic Items (if meaningful to you)

- ☐ Candle of remembrance
- ☐ Small plant or flower
- ☐ Religious or spiritual symbol

☐ Feather, seashell, or token found during a walk

☐ Journal for reflection or prayers

Step 3: Add Words That Heal

Include affirmations or comforting phrases to remind you that love remains.

You can write them on cards, sticky notes, or a chalkboard near your space.

Affirmation Ideas:

☐ "I did my best, and my love was enough."

☐ "Peace fills the space where pain once lived."

☐ "Love never ends—it changes form."

☐ "My pet's memory lives gently in my heart."

☐ "I give myself permission to rest and to heal."

☐ "Even though my heart aches, I honor the love that remains."

My personal affirmation:

Step 4: Create a Ritual of Use

Choose one or two ways to use your Comfort Corner regularly:

☐ Light a candle each morning or evening

☐ Sit quietly and breathe for one minute when you feel overwhelmed

☐ Write a letter to your pet or a gratitude note each week

☐ Listen to calming music when triggers appear

☐ Hold a keepsake and say, "Thank you for your love."

My Comfort Corner Ritual:

Step 5: Reflection

"This space is my reminder that grief is love seeking a place to land."

How do you feel when you sit in your Comfort Corner?

What do you want this space to remind you of?

The Daily Remembrance Practice

Ritual

Grief can feel like an ache that never fully quiets — a constant reminder of what's missing. Yet love, when gently tended, can transform that ache into connection. This ritual helps you create a peaceful daily moment to honor your pet's ongoing presence in your heart. Over time, these small acts of remembrance help retrain your nervous system to associate memory with calm, gratitude, and love instead of pain.

Instructions

Choose Your Moment:

Select a consistent time each day — morning as you wake, or evening before bed.

This one minute pause is your sacred space for remembrance. It doesn't need to be elaborate — just intentional.

Create the Connection:

Light a candle, step outside into the open air, or hold your pet's photo, collar, or another meaningful item in your hands.

Feel the texture, the warmth, the memory it carries. Allow your breath to slow and your body to soften.

Speak Aloud or Silently Within:

"You are still part of my day.

Your love still lives within me.

I carry your spirit in the quiet moments between my breaths."

If you prefer, you can say the original simple phrase — "You are still part of my day."

What matters most is the sincerity behind the words.

Let the Feeling Settle:

As you breathe, imagine your heart remembering love rather than loss.

The goal is not to "move on" — but to gently retrain your body and mind to experience remembrance as comfort instead of pain.

With time, this practice weaves your pet's memory into your daily rhythm, helping you feel less fractured and more whole.

Close the Moment:

Extinguish the candle, whisper thank you, or simply smile.

Carry the warmth of that connection with you throughout the day or into your dreams.

Reflection

How did it feel to include my pet in today's rhythm?

What emotion arose as I remembered them with calm instead of sorrow?

Affirmation

"The space that feels empty is filled with love."

End-of-Chapter Check-In Self-Assessment Questions

1. Have I noticed which moments of my day are hardest — and why?

2. Did I try one new coping tool that brought relief or calm?

3. Do I feel a little more at peace sitting with silence?

Chapter Four

Paw Prints of Love

Honoring Memory & Meaning

Welcome back, friend.

You've walked through the hardest parts — understanding your grief, releasing guilt, and learning to live with the quiet. This chapter is about love — not as something lost, but as something transformed. You don't "let go" of a pet you love; you learn to hold on differently. It's my hope this chapter will help you reconnect with your pet through memory, ritual, and creativity — turning your grief into a living tribute of love.

Continuing Bonds: A Modern Approach to Healing After Loss

For many years, grief was thought of as a process of letting go—of severing emotional ties with the one who died in order to move on. But modern psychology tells a different story. We now understand that healthy healing often involves continuing bonds—maintaining an enduring sense of connection, love, and meaning even after physical separation. In this approach, healing does not mean forgetting. It means finding new ways to carry love forward.

What Are Continuing Bonds?

The Continuing Bonds Theory (Klass, Silverman, & Nickman, 1996) emerged from research showing that many bereaved individuals continue to feel connected to their loved ones—and that this can be a healthy, adaptive part of grief.

A continuing bond might look like:

- Talking to your pet out loud or in your thoughts

- Keeping photos or mementos in your home

- Saying good morning or good night to them

- Feeling their presence in dreams or quiet moments

- Volunteering, donating, or helping animals in their honor

- Living by values your pet taught you—kindness, patience, joy

These actions aren't signs of "not moving on."

 They're signs that your heart is integrating the loss into a new reality.

Why Ongoing Connection Helps

Love is a neural and emotional pattern that the brain learns and repeats. Your relationship with your pet shaped your nervous system through shared routines, affection, and mutual safety. When your pet dies, the physical relationship ends—but the emotional and neurological imprint remains. By intentionally nurturing positive memories and ongoing rituals of remembrance, you help your brain and body reestablish safety, continuity, and peace. This turns grief from something that feels like endless absence into a relationship that continues to give meaning and comfort.

Healthy Continuing Bonds vs. Painful Clinging

It's natural to revisit memories and to wish for more time. But when grief becomes consumed by guilt, denial, or avoidance, those same bonds can feel heavy instead of healing.

Healthy Continuing | *Bonds Painful Clinging*

Memories bring warmth or comfort | *Memories trigger distress or self-blame*

Rituals feel grounding | *Rituals feel obsessive or obligatory*

Connection inspires action or gratitude | *Connection prevents daily functioning*

"I miss you, but I carry you with me." | *"I can't go on without you."*

If your connection feels more painful than peaceful, it may help to talk about it in counseling, where you can reshape the bond into one that nurtures rather than drains you.

Ways to Nurture Continuing Bonds

Try one or two of these gentle practices:

☐ Light a candle each week in remembrance

☐ Keep one of your pet's toys or tags in a special place

☐ Write a "message of the day" in your journal to them

☐ Visit a favorite walking path or park and say their name aloud

☐ Volunteer or donate in their memory

☐ Create a ritual of gratitude—thanking them for a lesson they taught you

A Closing Thought

"The goal is not to let go, but to grow—

to find a new way to hold the love that never left."

Grief is love that must learn a new language.

Every time you remember your pet with kindness instead of pain, you are speaking that language—and continuing a bond that no loss can erase.

Journal Prompt:

"What does my love for my pet look like now, in this new form?"

The Continuing Bonds Model of Grief

For generations, people were taught that healing from loss meant letting go—that to "move on," one had to detach completely from the person or pet who had died. Grief was often framed as a linear process that ended with acceptance and separation. But modern grief research, especially through the Continuing Bonds Model, has shown something profoundly different: real healing happens not by severing connection, but by maintaining it. Love does not disappear with physical absence; it changes form and finds new ways to exist.

Continuing bonds means allowing your relationship with your pet to evolve beyond the physical world. It's perfectly healthy and normal to talk to your pet, to sense their presence in familiar spaces, or to include them in rituals and moments of reflection. Lighting a candle in their honor, saying goodnight before bed, or keeping a favorite photo nearby are all ways love continues to flow. These actions are not signs of denial—they're expressions of an ongoing relationship that now lives within your memory, your habits, and your heart.

This approach honors the truth that grief and love are intertwined. The pain you feel is a reflection of the depth of your bond, and by nurturing that bond in new ways, you begin to integrate loss into your life rather than trying to erase it. Healing, then, becomes less about closure and more about transformation—about carrying your pet's love forward into the person you are becoming.

Exercise:

Take a few moments to write a short letter to your pet that begins with:

"Even though you're not here in body, you're still with me when..."

Let your words flow freely. Maybe you feel them in the warmth of the morning sun, the quiet comfort of bedtime, or the wag of another dog's tail that reminds you of their joy. Each memory, each moment of connection, is a thread in the tapestry of love that continues to live on—unbroken, evolving, and forever yours.

How Continuing Bonds Support Emotional Healing

Love Doesn't End—It Evolves. When we lose a beloved pet, it may feel as if love itself has been taken away. Yet the truth is: the love remains. It simply changes form. The concept of continuing bonds reminds us that our connection with our pet can still exist in new, meaningful ways. Healing doesn't come from forgetting or moving on—it comes from remembering with tenderness instead of pain. "Love is not broken by loss. It transforms into memory, meaning, and presence."

Grief is the mind's and body's way of adapting to absence. Your nervous system, habits, and emotions were all shaped by daily interactions with your pet—feeding, walking, cuddling, or simply sharing space. When that connection is disrupted, your brain seeks ways to restore the pattern of love. Continuing bonds help fulfill this need by maintaining emotional contact in healthy, soothing ways. They give the nervous system and heart a new sense of stability, safety, and belonging.

Examples of Continuing Bonds

• Speaking to your pet during quiet moments or prayer

• Keeping a photo, tag, or paw print nearby

• Creating a ritual of lighting a candle or saying goodnight

• Writing letters or journal entries to your pet

• Donating or volunteering in their memory

• Living by the values they taught you—loyalty, joy, unconditional love

None of these actions "trap" you in grief; instead, they give your love a new rhythm.

What Healing Feels Like

At first, memories may bring tears. Over time, those same memories bring warmth and gratitude. This is emotional healing in action—the gradual shift from ache to appreciation.

Healthy continuing bonds help you:

- Feel connected instead of alone

- Remember your pet with peace instead of guilt

- Carry their love into new relationships and experiences

A Reflection Exercise

"My love continues through the way I live."

Write one or two ways you feel your pet's presence today:

Complete the sentence:

"Because of my pet, I now…"

Continuing bonds are not a sign that you can't move forward—they are evidence that love has taken root deep enough to guide you through the rest of your life. Your grief is the proof of your love. Your healing is the proof that love endures.

Memory as Medicine

Memories are the mind's natural way of keeping love alive. In the early stages of grief, they can feel sharp—like touching something beautiful and broken at the same time. A familiar sound, a photo, or a remembered routine may bring an ache to the chest or tears to the eyes. But over time, these same memories begin to soften. They shift from being reminders of loss to gentle sources of comfort. From a psychological and physiological perspective, remembering can actually help heal. Revisiting positive memories of your pet activates parts of the brain that release soothing neurochemicals, calming the nervous system and reducing the body's stress response. In this way, memory becomes a form of medicine—helping you reconnect with warmth, safety, and gratitude instead of only pain.

The goal is not to stop remembering, but to remember with peace. Each recollection is a thread that keeps your pet's spirit woven into your life in a healthy, loving way. The more you engage with memories consciously and compassionately, the more your brain begins to associate your pet not only with loss but with love, joy, and the gifts they left behind.

Journal Prompt

List five memories of your pet that make you smile. Describe what each one taught you about love, loyalty, or joy. Maybe it's the way they greeted you at the door, the sound of their paws on the floor, or the quiet comfort of their presence beside you. Let these moments unfold vividly on the page—each one a small act of healing.

Reflection

When I revisit these memories, what happens in my body—tension, softness, warmth? Notice the sensations that arise. Do you feel your shoulders release, your breath deepen, or your heart expand just a little? These are signs that your body remembers love, too—that the connection between you and your pet lives on, not only in thought, but in every fiber of your being.

Creating Meaning After Loss

In the aftermath of loss, one of the most powerful forms of healing comes from meaning-making—the process of transforming pain into purpose. Meaning-making doesn't deny grief or rush it; instead, it allows us to hold sorrow and growth in the same heart. It's how we take something that once broke us and use it to build compassion, empathy, and gratitude. When we search for meaning after the death of a beloved pet, we begin to integrate their presence into the ongoing story of our lives. Their absence stops being a void and becomes a source of quiet strength—a reminder of how deeply we are capable of loving.

To begin this process, ask yourself: What did my pet teach me about life? How did they change who I am? How can I express their legacy through the way I live or love others? Each answer reveals how your connection continues, not in memory alone but in action. Maybe your pet taught you patience, forgiveness, or unconditional love. Maybe they showed you how to slow down and appreciate the simple joys of sunlight, fresh air, and affection. Perhaps their trust, humor, or resilience awakened something in you that remains long after their physical presence is gone.

Meaning-making doesn't erase pain—it gives it direction. It turns grief into movement, love into legacy. The lessons your pet offered through their companionship now live within you, waiting to be shared with the world in new ways.

Exercise:

Complete this sentence in your journal:

"Because I loved [pet's name], I now..."

Let your response come from the heart. You might write, "Because I loved Lacey, I now pause to appreciate simple moments." Or, "Because I loved Max, I now support animal rescues." Or, "Because I loved Bella, I am kinder to others who are hurting." Each statement transforms memory into meaning—proof that love, when truly lived, never ends. It simply changes form and continues through you.

Lessons of Love: Turning Memory Into Meaning

Activity

When someone we love passes—especially a beloved animal—our hearts often ache with both pain and gratitude. As time passes, many find that their grief gently begins to reveal lessons about love, compassion, patience, and resilience. This worksheet helps you explore what your pet taught you—and how their memory continues to shape who you are today. "We don't move on from love; we move forward with it."

Step 1: Remembering Their Gifts

Think about the unique qualities your pet brought into your life.

What words describe your pet's personality?

How did they show you love?

What small habits or quirks made you smile?

Step 2: Discovering the Lessons

Every pet teaches us something about life—and often, those lessons appear even more clearly in hindsight.

What did your pet teach you about unconditional love?

What did they teach you about patience, forgiveness, or living in the moment?

What lesson do you most want to carry forward into your daily life?

Step 3: Meaning From Memory

Turning memory into meaning doesn't mean letting go—it means allowing love to evolve into purpose.

How have you changed because of your bond with your pet?

In what ways can you honor them through your actions or choices?

Is there something you'd like to do in their memory? (e.g., volunteer, plant a tree, start a tradition)

Step 4: Rewriting the Story

Healing often means reframing the story of loss into one of continuing love.

Complete the sentence:

"Because of you, I now know that love can..."

Write a short note of gratitude to your pet:

"Thank you for teaching me..."

Step 5: Integration and Affirmation

Take a deep breath.

Feel your pet's presence in your heart, and read this affirmation aloud—or write your own below:

"Your love still lives within me.

I honor your memory through the way I love, care, and live each day.

Our bond continues in every act of kindness and compassion I share."

My personal affirmation:

Reflection Prompt

"Love's greatest lesson is that it never truly leaves—it becomes who we are."

In your own words, what has your pet's love taught you about being human?

Legacy Craft Tutorial

Activity

Creating a memorial for your pet is a deeply personal and healing experience. It doesn't have to be grand or complicated—what matters is that it comes from the heart. Memorializing your pet gives your love a place to go. It allows your hands to create something tangible from something invisible, transforming grief into a living expression of remembrance. Whether your creation is simple or detailed, the act of crafting becomes a gentle ritual of connection—one that honors your pet's presence in your life and keeps their memory close.

You might choose to make something simple, like lighting a candle beside a favorite photo or writing a few lines of poetry that capture your pet's spirit. Or you could create a small scrapbook or collage that tells the story of your time together—filled with photos, little notes, and maybe even a lock of fur or a tag. Another beautiful option is a memory jar: find a small jar or box and fill it with written memories, moments that make you smile, or things you want to remember forever. Whenever a memory surfaces, add it to the jar. Over time, it becomes a treasure chest of love and gratitude you can revisit whenever you need comfort.

If you enjoy creative projects, consider framing your pet's name, pawprint, or favorite quote alongside a photograph. You could even press flowers from a place you loved walking together or include small keepsakes that symbolize their personality. None of these projects have to be perfect; they are simply extensions of your love.

Every act of remembrance is an act of love. When you create with intention, you are giving shape to something eternal—the bond between you and your pet. Through art, ritual, and memory, their spirit continues to live on in your hands, your heart, and the quiet beauty of the life you keep building around their love.

***

Step 1: Choose a Project That Resonates

Select one or more keepsakes that feel meaningful to you.

(You don't have to be "crafty." This is about connection, not perfection.)

Project Idea Materials You'll Need Symbolic Meaning

Memory Candle

Candle, photo, glass jar, label or engraving pen Light as remembrance, warmth as love's endurance

Shadow Box

Small frame box, photos, collar/tag, flowers, note A visual story of your bond and shared life

Memory Stone or Garden Marker

Smooth stone, paint pen or engraving, sealer Grounding and remembrance in nature

Photo Collage or Scrapbook Page

Printed photos, paper, glue, quotes Honoring milestones and joyful memories

Fabric Keepsake or Pillow

Piece of blanket or toy fabric, sewing kit Comfort and continued closeness

Paw Print Ornament

Clay or plaster, ribbon, imprint tool Tangible connection to your pet's presence

Digital Slideshow or Video Tribute

Music, photos, video clips Sharing love and story with others

Plant or Tree Dedication

Seedling, soil, pot, marker Growth, renewal, and life continuing forward

Which project(s) call to you?

Step 2: Gather Materials

Make a list of what you'll need before starting.

Include sentimental items, textures, or colors that remind you of your pet.

My material list:

Step 3: Create With Intention

Before you begin, pause and take three slow breaths.

Say aloud or silently:

"I create this in love and remembrance. May it bring comfort and peace."

As you work:

• Play gentle music

• Light a candle or use calming scents (lavender, sandalwood)

• Allow emotions to rise without judgment—tears, smiles, and silence all belong here

• If it feels right, speak your pet's name or share a favorite memory as you create

Step 4: Add Personal Touches

Consider including:

☐ Your pet's name or nickname

☐ A paw print, photo, or tag

☐ A favorite quote or mantra

☐ Dried flowers from their favorite spot

☐ A note or letter sealed within the project

☐ A symbol of peace (heart, feather, star, or rainbow)

Notes about what I plan to include:

Step 5: Display or Dedicate Your Creation

Find a special place to keep or display your memorial item:

☐ On your Comfort Corner shelf

☐ Near a candle or framed photo

☐ In your garden or outdoor sanctuary

☐ In a memory box or keepsake drawer

Say a few words of dedication, such as:

"This is for you, my friend. Thank you for every moment of love. Your memory lives here."

Where I'll place or dedicate my keepsake:

Step 6: Reflection

After creating your project, spend a few minutes journaling:

How did I feel before, during, and after creating this memorial?

What did this process teach me about my grief or love?

Optional Group or Family Activity

Invite family members (including children) to create their own mini keepsakes. This can promote shared healing, open communication, and mutual remembrance. Each project becomes a small piece of a larger legacy of love.

Memorial projects are not about replacing your pet—they are about expressing love that continues to grow. Every candle, stone, or photo tells a story of connection that time cannot erase. "What we once held in our arms, we now carry in our hearts."

Embracing Memory
Guided Meditation

Find a comfortable position where you can relax without strain.
Let your shoulders soften, your jaw unclench, and your breathing settle into an easy rhythm.

If it feels comforting, place a hand over your heart.
Feel its warmth.
Feel your pulse — the steady rhythm of life continuing within you.

Today's meditation is about *remembering* — not to reopen pain, but to honor love.
Each memory is a thread that connects your heart to theirs.
Together, those threads create the tapestry of your shared life — woven with laughter, comfort, loyalty, and presence.

Take a deep breath in...
and exhale gently.
Let your heart open to memory.

The Memory Garden

Imagine that you are standing before a quiet garden gate.
The air is soft and warm.
You can hear the gentle sound of water and the whisper of leaves.

As you open the gate, you step into a garden that feels familiar —

a sacred place where every flower, every sound, every scent holds a piece of your shared story.

The sunlight filters through the trees, creating patterns of gold on the path ahead.
You walk slowly, breathing in the calm air.
Each step brings forward a memory — not rushed, not forced — simply appearing like petals opening to the light.

You see the places you played together,
the moments they greeted you at the door,
the times they rested quietly by your side when words weren't needed.

You might smile. You might cry.
Both are welcome here.
This garden exists beyond time, tended by love.

The Heart's Reflection

In the center of the garden, you find a small, clear pond.
The surface is still, mirroring the sky above.

As you look into the water, you see reflections — not of grief, but of connection.
You see the joy you gave one another,

the comfort you shared in moments of pain,
the lessons your pet taught you about loyalty, presence, and unconditional love.

Allow your heart to whisper:

"Thank you for loving me.
Thank you for choosing me."

As you breathe, notice how the pond begins to shimmer with light —
the light of remembrance transforming sorrow into peace.

Integrating the Bond

Now imagine that this golden light rises gently from the pond and flows into your heart.
It carries every memory — every tail wag, every purr, every moment of companionship —
and settles deep within your chest, glowing softly.

You realize now: nothing has truly been lost.
It has only changed form.

Their spirit continues to live within you —
in the way you care,
the way you notice small joys,
the way your heart opens to love again.

Breathe deeply, letting this light fill you completely.
You are whole, even in grief.
You are healing, even as you remember.

Resting in Gratitude

Take a few moments now to rest in quiet gratitude.
You may whisper softly:

"I carry your love in my heart.
Our bond is eternal."

Feel the warmth of gratitude soften your body,
the peace of remembrance calm your mind,
and the love between you radiate like sunlight through the trees.

You are not alone.
You never have been.
Love endures, even as the form changes.

Returning from the Garden

When you're ready, begin walking back toward the gate.
Turn once more to look behind you.
The garden remains — blooming, living, sacred.
A place you can return to any time you wish to feel close again.

Step through the gate and close it gently.
Carry the warmth of this memory garden within you.
Carry the peace of connection wherever you go.

Take one final deep breath in through your nose...
and exhale softly through your mouth.

When you're ready, open your eyes.
You are here, now — with a heart both tender and strong.

Closing Affirmation

"I honor the love we shared.
I release the pain, but keep the light.
Through memory, love lives on."

The Legacy of Love Ceremony

Ritual

This ceremony marks the moment when your love transforms from presence to legacy. It honors the truth that your pet's life continues to shape yours — in your kindness, your memories, your choices, and your heart. This is not an ending, but an evolution: the love you once gave outward now becomes a light you carry within.

Prepare Your Space

Choose a quiet place that feels meaningful — indoors with a candle, or outdoors under the open sky.

You may wish to bring photos, toys, a collar, or other keepsakes that symbolize your bond.

If possible, set out a small bowl of water or a single flower — representing life continuing in gentle ways.

Center Yourself

Take several slow breaths.

With each inhale, feel your chest expand with gratitude.

With each exhale, release the heaviness that still clings to your loss.

When you feel ready, light your candle and let your gaze rest on its steady flame.

Speak or Read Aloud

"Your love changed me.

It softened my edges and opened my heart.

The lessons you taught me — patience, joy, loyalty, presence —

I now carry forward into the world.

This is your legacy of love, living through me."

Take a moment to reflect on how your pet's presence shaped you.

You might name one quality you wish to continue in their honor — perhaps gentleness, curiosity, or resilience.

Create a Symbol of Legacy

Write your pet's name and the word or quality you chose on a small piece of paper.

You can:

o Burn it safely in the candle's flame, releasing the smoke skyward as a message of love.

o Bury it beneath a tree or plant it with a flower seed.

o Keep it in your journal or memory box as a vow to carry that love forward.

Whatever you choose, let it represent a promise — that your pet's spirit will continue to ripple through your life.

Close the Ceremony

Place your hand over your heart.

Whisper a simple truth:

"Your story lives in me."

Blow out the candle slowly, watching the smoke rise like a bridge between worlds.

Sit for a few moments in gratitude, feeling the peace of love transformed.

Reflection

What quality or lesson from my pet's life do I wish to carry forward as part of their legacy?

How might I express that love in my daily life?

Affirmation

"Love doesn't end — it changes form. I carry my pet's light within me."

End-of-Chapter Check-In:

1. Have I found new ways to remember my pet with peace instead of pain?

2. Do I feel more connected to them when I engage in creative remembrance?

3. What meaning or lesson from their life do I want to carry forward?

Chapter Five

Permission to Heal

Reconnecting With Life

Welcome back, friend.

You've carried your grief with such courage. You've honored your pet's memory and discovered ways to keep their love alive. In this chapter, we'll explore something many people find both beautiful and hard — letting life back in. Sometimes, joy feels disloyal after loss. But feeling joy again doesn't mean forgetting; it means your heart is growing strong enough to hold both sorrow and love. In this chapter, you'll practice opening your heart to small moments of peace, gratitude, and connection — without guilt.

Allowing Joy While Grieving

For many who have loved and lost a pet, joy can feel like betrayal. You might catch yourself laughing and suddenly feel a pang of guilt—"How can I smile when they're gone?" This is one of grief's quietest burdens: the belief that healing means you've stopped caring. But joy does not erase love. It is proof that love has changed shape—that the heart, even after breaking, is learning to beat freely again.

Understanding Emotional Duality

Grief and joy are not opposites; they are companions.

Our minds often think in "either/or"—either I'm grieving or I'm okay. But emotions are layered, and healing happens in both/and:

• You can cry one moment and laugh the next.

• You can miss your pet deeply and still feel peace.

• You can honor their memory while embracing new beginnings.

The presence of joy doesn't mean the absence of love; it means your love has found new ways to breathe.

Why Joy Is Part of Healing

From a psychological perspective, grief activates both pain and attachment systems in the brain. When we engage in activities that bring pleasure or calm—walking, connecting, creating—we stimulate the same areas that were once activated through love and play with our pets. Joyful moments help regulate the nervous system, allowing your body to move from survival mode to safety. They don't diminish the bond; they sustain it.

Granting Yourself Permission

It takes courage to let light back in. You are not leaving your pet behind—you are carrying them forward into every warm moment you allow yourself to feel. "I can remember with love and still live with joy." Each smile, each gentle laugh, each step toward peace is a continuation of your story together—not an ending.

Reflection

When I feel joy, what story do I tell myself about what it means?

What would my pet want for me right now?

How might joy honor their memory instead of replace it?

A Closing Thought

"Healing doesn't mean forgetting.

It means remembering with more love than pain."

You have permission to laugh.

You have permission to rest.

You have permission to live fully, carrying their love within you.

Joy is not the end of grief—it's the light that guides you through it.

Journal Prompt

"What's one thing that has brought me even a tiny moment of comfort since my pet's passing?"

Why Joy Feels Scary After Loss

After a deep loss, joy can feel almost impossible—and when it does begin to return, it can feel frightening. Many grieving pet parents find themselves caught in an emotional tug-of-war: part of them wants to smile or laugh again, while another part whispers, "If I feel happy, I'm forgetting. If I move on, I'm betraying." This internal conflict is common. The heart associates sorrow with love, as if mourning is the only way to stay connected. Yet true love is not measured by suffering. Your grief honors your bond, but so does your capacity for joy.

Grief and joy are not opposites—they are companions. Both arise from the same source: love. The deeper you loved, the deeper the ache of loss, but also the greater the capacity for joy when your heart begins to heal. Allowing yourself to experience moments of peace, laughter, or lightness does not mean you are leaving your pet behind. It means you are carrying them forward—letting their love become the reason you continue to live fully. When you laugh again, you are not betraying your pet; you are honoring the life and joy they brought into yours.

Remember, your pet's happiness came from seeing you alive, engaged, and whole. They didn't measure your love by tears—they felt it in your presence, your care, your companionship. They would not want your world to grow dim in their absence. They would want their legacy to be light: you, living with the same warmth, curiosity, and love they gave so freely.

Exercise:

Open your journal and make two lists. First, write down the things that make you feel guilty for feeling happy again—maybe it's smiling at another animal, enjoying a sunny day, or laughing with friends. Then, on the second list, ask yourself: What might my pet say about that guilt? Imagine their spirit responding with the unconditional love they always offered. Chances are, they would want you to release that guilt and let joy return, because joy is how their love continues to live through you.

When we grieve, we often extend compassion to everyone around us — family members, friends, even strangers who mean well — yet we rarely offer that same tenderness to ourselves. You may have comforted others who were hurting, reassured loved ones that they did enough, or soothed your pet with unconditional love during their final days. But have you spoken to yourself that way? Grief often awakens an inner critic that says you should be coping better, crying less, or moving on faster. Self-compassion is the antidote to that voice. It means acknowledging your pain without judgment and remembering that being human means being imperfect and tender all at once.

Self-Compassion in Action

Self-compassion asks you to treat yourself with the same gentleness you showed your pet—the same tone of voice, the same patience, the same understanding. It's recognizing that you are grieving because you loved deeply, and that love deserves kindness, not criticism. When you soften toward yourself, the edges of grief become easier to hold. You stop fighting the pain and begin to hold it with care.

Mini-Practice:

Find a quiet place where you can sit without distraction. Close your eyes and rest one hand over your heart. Say aloud, slowly and sincerely:

"This hurts. I am doing my best. I deserve kindness."

Take three deep, intentional breaths. With each exhale, imagine warmth radiating outward from your heart—soft, steady, and healing. Feel it spread through your chest, down your arms, and into your body. Let it remind you that you are still alive, still capable of love, and still worthy of gentleness.

Reflection

When I speak to myself kindly, what changes in how I feel?

Notice whether your breath deepens, your shoulders relax, or your chest feels a little lighter. Self-compassion may not erase grief, but it changes the way grief lives within you. It transforms suffering into tenderness and reminds you that healing begins not with perfection—but with kindness.

Reconnecting Through the Senses

Grief has a way of narrowing the world. Colors fade, sounds dull, and even the simplest pleasures can lose their meaning. When you're grieving, the body often mirrors the heart's withdrawal—your senses shut down as a form of protection, trying to shield you from further pain. But healing begins when you gently reawaken those senses. By allowing yourself to truly feel the world again—sunlight on your skin, the smell of rain, the sound of birdsong, or the taste of something you love—you remind your nervous system that life is still here. It hasn't gone anywhere; it's been waiting patiently to meet you again, one small moment at a time.

Each sensory experience is like a tiny thread pulling you back into connection with the present. When you notice warmth, texture, or beauty, you're sending signals of safety to your body—inviting calm after the storm of grief. These sensations don't erase sadness, but they create space for balance. You begin to realize that pain and peace can coexist, just as love and loss do. Reconnecting with your senses helps bridge that gap, allowing the world to expand again around you.

Exercise:

Try taking a mindful walk or simply sitting outdoors for five quiet minutes. With each breath, turn your attention to the present moment. Notice one thing you can see that feels beautiful—perhaps the way light filters through leaves or the shape of a cloud. Listen for one sound that feels soothing—a soft breeze, the hum of life around you. Notice one smell that feels comforting—fresh air, flowers, or earth after rain. Finally, pay attention to one sensation on your skin that feels grounding—the warmth of the sun, the coolness of shade, or the gentle weight of your clothing.

When you finish, write down what you noticed and how it made you feel. Did your breath slow? Did something inside you soften, even briefly? These sensory moments remind you that while loss changes everything, the world still offers quiet invitations to stay connected—to life, to love, and to yourself.

Allowing Light Back In
Activity

After losing a beloved pet, many people struggle with the belief that feeling happy means forgetting—or worse, betraying—the one they lost. But love and grief are not opposites. Your ability to feel joy again is not a sign that your love has ended; it's proof that it still lives within you. This activity helps you explore where guilt may be blocking your healing—and how to gently replace it with permission, gratitude, and peace. "I can miss you and still smile. That is how love survives loss."

Step 1: Identify the Belief

Think of a moment when you felt joy, peace, or laughter—and then guilt immediately followed.

What happened?

What thought came up right after?

How did that thought make you feel (emotionally and physically)?

Step 2: Name the Guilt Story

Write down what your guilt is trying to tell you.

Sometimes guilt speaks in hidden messages—like "You shouldn't be okay," or "If you smile, you didn't love them enough."

My guilt says:

If I were to translate that into truth, what might it actually mean?

(Example: "I miss them so much, and I don't want life to move on without them.")

Step 3: Reframe the Belief

Now, replace the guilt with a truth that honors both your love and your right to heal.

Old Thought New Reframe

"If I'm happy, it means I've forgotten." "My happiness is part of the love I carry forward."

"Moving on means leaving them behind." "I'm not moving on—I'm moving forward with their memory."

"They deserved my sadness." "They deserve to be remembered with joy."

Write your own reframe:

Step 4: Remember What They Would Want for You

Imagine your pet could see you right now.

What would they want for your days ahead?

My pet would want me to...

When I smile or laugh, they would probably think...

"If they could speak, they would say: I'm still with you. Keep living. Keep loving."

Step 5: Invite Joy Gently

List small ways you can welcome light back into your days—without guilt, without pressure.

☐ Taking a walk in nature

☐ Lighting a candle in their honor

☐ Smiling at a memory

☐ Playing music they loved

☐ Spending time with other animals

☐ Writing a letter of gratitude

☐ Other:

Today, I will allow myself one moment of joy by:

Step 6: Affirmation

Read this aloud—or write your own version:

"Feeling joy does not mean I've forgotten.

It means my love has learned how to shine through the pain.

I honor my pet's memory by choosing to live fully and kindly, as they taught me."

My personal affirmation:

Reflection

"Joy is the way love breathes after loss."

You do not need to earn the right to heal.

You already have permission to feel peace, laughter, and warmth again.

These emotions are not the end of your grief—they are the continuation of your love.

Mindful Senses

Activity

Grief can pull us out of the present moment. You might feel detached from your surroundings, trapped in memories, or unable to focus. These sensations are part of how the nervous system protects itself after loss—by going numb or seeking escape from pain. Mindful sensory grounding helps bring your body back into safety and awareness. It reminds you that you are still here, and that comfort, beauty, and connection can still be experienced right now. "When grief disconnects you from the world, your senses can gently lead you home."

Step 1: Find a Quiet Moment

Sit or stand somewhere calm.

Take a slow breath in through your nose, and exhale through your mouth.

Allow yourself to pause—not to fix anything, but to feel where you are in this moment.

Step 2: See

Look around your space. Notice five things you can see. They can be colors, shapes, or objects that bring even a small sense of peace.

1.

2.

3.

4.

5.

Which of these feels comforting or beautiful to you?

Step 3: Hear

Listen carefully. Notice four sounds around you—soft or distant, natural or manmade.

1.

2.

3.

4.

Which sound feels grounding or soothing?

Step 4: Touch

Notice three things you can touch or feel right now.

It could be the texture of your clothing, a blanket, your pet's collar, or the surface beneath your hand.

1.

2.

3.

Which texture feels the safest or most comforting?

Step 5: Smell

Take a slow breath in through your nose. Notice two scents—pleasant, neutral, or meaningful.

If possible, light a candle, hold a flower, or use a calming essential oil.

1.

2.

Is there a scent that reminds you of your pet or a peaceful memory?

Step 6: Taste

Notice one thing you can taste right now.

This could be a sip of water, a cup of tea, or even just the air in your mouth.

1.

If you could taste a memory with your pet, what would it be? (e.g., a picnic, morning coffee, a treat you shared)

Step 7: Reflection

Take another slow breath.

Notice any shifts in your body—less tension, slower breathing, more awareness.

How do you feel now compared to when you began this exercise?

Which sense helps you feel most grounded when grief feels heavy?

"Grief lives in the body, but so does healing."

Each time you reconnect to your senses, you remind your nervous system that it is safe to rest, to feel, and to begin again.

Letter From Your Pet

Activity

Writing a letter from your pet's perspective can be one of the most comforting and healing exercises during grief. It allows you to reconnect with their love, not as something lost, but as something still present—something that continues to speak through memory, emotion, and intuition. This gentle writing practice invites you to shift from pain to presence, giving your heart permission to hear your pet's voice once more.

Find a quiet place where you can be still and undisturbed for a few minutes. Take a deep breath and close your eyes. Picture your pet as you remember them at their happiest—healthy, playful, and full of life. See their eyes bright with affection, their body relaxed and content. Feel the warmth of that familiar energy surrounding you. Then, imagine what they would say to you if they could speak to you today. Don't overthink or censor your thoughts. Simply let their love come through your words. You may find the message flows easily, or you might pause and cry along the way—both are perfectly okay.

Begin your letter with the prompt:

"Dear [Your Name], thank you for every day you loved me. I was happiest when..."

From there, let the words take shape as if your pet were writing directly to you. Maybe they'd remind you of how much they adored your voice, your laughter, your touch. Perhaps they'd tell you that they never felt alone or afraid because they always had you. They might even reassure you that you did enough, that they are at peace, and that they still feel connected to you, just in a new way.

As you write, allow whatever emotions surface to move through you. Tears, smiles, or a mix of both—these are signs of love being released, transformed, and remembered. You can get inspiration from the template below.

Reflection:

When you finish, take a moment to notice what emotions arose while writing. Did any part of the exercise feel healing, freeing, or surprising? Did you sense your pet's presence more vividly? This practice is not about imagination alone—it's about deep listening. The words that appear on the page are often the ones your heart most needs to hear. Through this process, love speaks again, reminding you that while their body is gone, their spirit remains—always near, always loving, always yours.

Letter From My Pet Template

Dear [Your Name],

(Imagine your pet's loving voice — gentle, familiar, and kind.)

Prompts to Guide You

If you're not sure where to begin, try completing a few of these thoughts in your pet's voice:

- "I want you to know that I felt..."
- "When I was with you, my favorite thing was..."
- "Please stop worrying about..."
- "Even though you can't see me, I'm still..."
- "You helped me feel safe when..."
- "What I loved most about our time together was..."
- "When you think of me, remember..."
- "You didn't fail me. You gave me..."
- "When you laugh again, I'll be..."
- "You will always carry me in your..."

Love Always,

[Your Pet's Name]

Optional: attach a favorite photo of your pet to the letter.

Reflection

Take a moment to read what you've written.

Notice the emotions that arise — warmth, tears, calm, or gratitude.

This letter is your pet's legacy of love, spoken through your heart.

What did you feel or realize as you wrote this letter?

"The words you write are not make-believe — they are love translated into language."

Light Returning
Guided Meditation

Take a comfortable position, somewhere you can rest without interruption.

You may sit, lie down, or place a hand over your heart.

Close your eyes.

Take a deep breath in through your nose...

and exhale slowly through your mouth.

Let your shoulders drop.

Let your jaw soften.

Let your heart begin to settle.

There's nothing to fix, nothing to do.

Just this moment.

Just your breath.

Visualizing the Heart

Now, imagine your heart as a window that's been closed for a while.

It's not broken—just resting, waiting for the right time to open again.

As you inhale, picture soft light beginning to seep through the cracks.

It's gentle, golden, and warm—like the first morning sun touching a quiet room.

With each exhale, imagine that the window opens just a little wider.

The hinges move freely, the air feels lighter, and the light pours in more fully.

Receiving the Light

The light that fills you is love.

It's your love for your pet—pure, enduring, eternal—

and their love for you, flowing back without distance or time.

Feel it now:

A soft warmth blooming in your chest, spreading through your shoulders, arms, and fingertips.

It moves through your neck, down your spine, through your legs, and into your feet.

You are surrounded—completely held—in love's glow.

Love Remains

Let this light remind you: even in loss, love remains.

It changes form, but never disappears.

Whisper softly, or think the words in rhythm with your breath:

"I can feel love and joy again.

It's safe to live."

Repeat it once more, slower this time—

letting each word settle gently into your body:

"I can feel love and joy again.

It's safe to live."

Closing

Take a few final breaths here, resting in the glow.

The window of your heart is open now—

not wide enough to overwhelm,

just enough to let love move freely once more.

You may notice a small smile, a warmth in your chest, or a quiet sense of ease.

Trust it. This is healing taking shape.

When you're ready, gently wiggle your fingers and toes.

Feel the surface beneath you.

Take one last deep breath in...

and exhale with a soft sigh.

Open your eyes.

The light has returned—and it will continue to grow.

Affirmation

"Grief softens, love remains, and my light returns—one breath at a time."

Moments of Softness
Ritual

By this stage in your healing, you've released guilt, welcomed remembrance, and begun to understand that love doesn't end — it transforms. This ritual invites you to reintroduce gentleness into your daily life. After the intensity of loss, the nervous system often remains guarded, braced against further pain. Moments of Softness help you reopen to safety, pleasure, and tenderness — one gentle moment at a time.

Create Your Soft Space:

Choose a space that feels comforting — a cozy chair, a patch of sunlight, or a quiet corner of your room.

You may bring a blanket, a candle, or an object that reminds you of your pet's warmth and presence.

This becomes your small sanctuary of safety.

Begin with Breath:

Take three slow, deliberate breaths.

With each inhale, imagine breathing in softness — light, warmth, compassion.

With each exhale, let go of tension, judgment, and the need to do anything.

Allow your shoulders to drop. Let your face relax. Feel your body soften into the present moment.

Invite Your Pet's Memory with Tenderness:

Think of a simple, joyful memory — perhaps the sound of their paws, the feeling of fur beneath your fingers, or the way their eyes met yours.

Instead of focusing on their absence, focus on the texture of love in that memory — the peace, playfulness, or calm it brought you.

Whisper softly:

"Your love taught me to be gentle.

I can still feel you in the quiet."

Anchor in Sensation:

Let the memory expand into the present through your senses.

o Notice the warmth of your hands or the light of the candle.

o Feel your breath move easily.

o Allow a half-smile if it wants to come.

These are the body's signals of safety returning. You are teaching yourself that remembering can coexist with calm.

Close with Gratitude:

Place your hand over your heart.

Say aloud or silently:

"Today I allowed myself to feel softness again.

My heart can hold both love and peace."

Blow out the candle (or simply close your eyes), feeling that soft energy linger in your chest — a quiet reminder that love, in its purest form, is never gone.

Reflection

What softened within me today?

How can I invite more gentleness — toward myself, others, and the memory of my pet — into my daily life?

Affirmation

"My heart can hold both love and loss. It is safe to live and to feel again."

End-of-Chapter Check-In:

1. Have I allowed myself to feel moments of peace or happiness without guilt?

2. Did I try speaking to myself with kindness and notice any change?

3. Do I feel more connected to the world around me this week?

Chapter Six

From Loss to Legacy
Moving Forward with Grace

Welcome back, my friend — and congratulations. You've shown courage, compassion, and vulnerability as you've walked through this book. Now, we reach the final step — not an ending, but a transformation. Love never disappears. It changes form, becoming part of who you are and how you move through the world. In this final chapter, we'll focus on gratitude, meaning, and legacy — carrying your pet's spirit forward with grace.

Understanding Integration: How Grief Becomes Growth

What Is Integration? Integration is the final phase of healing — not when grief disappears, but when it becomes part of you in a way that no longer feels overwhelming. It's when the love you shared and the pain you felt begin to coexist peacefully within your heart. In psychology, integration means bringing together all parts of an experience — the joy, the sorrow, the guilt, the gratitude — until they form a single, meaningful whole. Instead of asking "How do I move on?", integration asks: "How can I live forward with what this love has taught me?"

Healing as Transformation

Grief is not something we get over—it's something we grow through. Loss has a way of reshaping us from the inside out, changing the way we see the world, ourselves, and others. At first, it may feel as though something inside you has shattered beyond repair. The routines that once felt grounding now feel empty, and the person you were before the loss may seem unreachable. Yet, as time passes and tenderness begins to return, something remarkable happens: grief starts to carve space within you for greater compassion, empathy, and wisdom. It does not erase the love or the pain—it refines them into something new.

Healing through grief is a form of transformation. It softens hard edges and expands understanding. It allows you to recognize suffering in others and respond with more gentleness because you know what it feels like to ache. It teaches patience with yourself and gratitude for even the smallest joys—the smell of rain, the warmth of sunlight, the laughter of a loved one. The version of you who began this journey may have felt broken, but the version of you here now carries the strength, humility, and compassion that only love and loss could teach. You are not the same, and that is part of the gift.

Your healing is not about leaving your grief behind—it's about integrating it into who you've become. You carry your pet's love within you now, woven into the way you move through the world, the way you care for others, and the way you find meaning in ordinary moments. Grief, when met with courage and tenderness, becomes a quiet teacher that shapes the heart into something more expansive.

The Journey of Integration

In the beginning, grief feels like chaos — waves of emotion, unpredictable triggers, and sharp pain.

Over time, as you remember, cry, reflect, and rebuild, your nervous system learns that love can exist without physical presence.

You start to notice small signs of integration when:

• You can think of your pet and feel warmth instead of only pain.

• You can talk about them without tears every time.

• You find yourself helping others through their losses.

• You feel gratitude for the time you shared, even amid sadness.

• You realize their memory influences your choices and values today.

Integration isn't a moment—it's a gentle unfolding.

The Psychology of Growth Through Grief

Modern grief theory calls this process "meaning reconstruction."

It describes how, after a loss, people rebuild their identity and worldview to include both love and absence.

Your brain literally rewires itself to hold both:

• The pain of loss activates emotional processing centers.

- The act of remembrance stimulates areas linked to empathy, purpose, and connection.

- Over time, these networks merge, helping you carry your love as strength rather than sorrow.

This is what it means for grief to become growth:

You no longer live in the loss — you live through it, and beyond it.

Signs You Are Integrating

- You can reflect on your pet's life with both tears and smiles.

- You are curious about life again.

- You are finding new ways to express love—through care, creativity, or connection.

- You forgive yourself more easily.

- You sense that your pet's memory has become a part of who you are, not something separate or painful.

Which of these feel true for you today?

How to Support Integration

1. Reflect – Continue journaling, writing letters, or sharing stories.

2. Create Meaning – Engage in memorial projects or daily rituals of remembrance.

3. Connect – Talk with others who understand, or share your story to help someone else heal.

4. Embody the Lesson – Live out the qualities your pet taught you—loyalty, joy, gentleness, presence.

5. Allow Joy – Recognize that laughter, love, and peace are not betrayals; they are signs of integration.

"Healing doesn't mean you stop grieving. It means your grief has found a home inside your heart."

Reflection

How has your love for your pet changed or deepened since their passing?

What qualities or lessons do you carry forward into your daily life?

How will you honor this love through the way you live?

"Grief is not a wall to climb, but a garden to tend."

As you nurture your healing, the ache of loss transforms into wisdom, compassion, and grace. Integration is not the end of grief—it's the beginning of a new way of being. You will always carry your pet with you— not as pain, but as presence.

Journal Prompt:

"How have I changed since my pet's passing? What have I learned about myself, love, or life?"

Exercise:

Take a few moments to reflect on how you've changed since your loss. Write three statements that begin with:

"Because of my loss, I have learned..."

For example:

"Because of my loss, I have learned how strong I am."

"Because of my loss, I have learned to slow down and savor small moments."

"Because of my loss, I have learned that love never truly ends—it simply changes form."

As you write, notice how each sentence transforms pain into purpose. Healing is not a return to who you were; it is an evolution into someone deeper, wiser, and more open to life's fragile, beautiful balance between love and letting go.

How My Love Changed Me

Activity

Every bond we share with an animal shapes us in quiet and powerful ways. Love teaches us to care, to notice, to open our hearts. Loss, though painful, deepens that understanding—it refines how we live, love, and connect with others. This activity invites you to explore how your pet's love continues to live through you, influencing who you are today. "Grief changes you. But so does love."

Step 1: Remember the Love

What did your pet bring into your life that no one else could?

Describe one moment that captures the essence of your bond.

If you could describe your relationship in three words, what would they be?

Step 2: Recognize the Growth

Think about the person you were before your pet came into your life—and who you are now.

How did their love change the way you see the world?

What values or qualities did your pet help you strengthen (e.g., patience, empathy, playfulness, compassion)?

What have you learned about resilience through this experience?

Step 3: Integrate the Lessons

What lesson from your pet do you want to live by every day?

How can you express this lesson through your choices, relationships, or self-care?

If your pet could see you now, what do you think they'd be proud of?

Step 4: Create a "Love Legacy" Statement

Complete one or more of these sentences to define how your love continues to shape your life:

"Because of you, I now know…"

"Your love taught me to…"

"I will honor your memory by…"

"The world feels kinder because…"

Step 5: Reflection & Affirmation

Take a slow breath and place a hand over your heart.

Feel the warmth there — that's the love that remains.

How do you carry your pet's presence with you now?

What is one thing you want to thank them for today?

Affirmation

"Your love changed me forever.

I am softer, stronger, and more alive because of you."

My personalized affirmation:

Reflection

Integration doesn't mean letting go—it means recognizing that your heart has expanded.

The love you shared has become a part of your story, your compassion, and your purpose.

"What was once a single heartbeat between us now lives as rhythm within me."

Legacy in Action: Carrying Love Forward

A legacy is love in motion—it's how your pet's spirit continues to ripple outward through your life. When someone we love dies, especially a beloved animal companion, it can feel like their story ended too soon. But legacies remind us that love never truly stops; it just changes direction. Each act of kindness, compassion, and connection you share in their honor becomes a thread that keeps their presence alive in the world. A legacy doesn't have to be grand or public. It can be quiet, intimate, and deeply personal—a small gesture that reflects the bond you shared.

Perhaps your legacy looks like donating to a rescue organization or volunteering at a shelter. Maybe it's planting a garden filled with flowers that remind you of your pet or setting aside time each week to comfort someone else who's grieving. You might write a story, paint a picture, or compose a piece of music inspired by them. Even simple choices—like living with more patience, adopting another animal when you're ready, or offering kindness to a stranger—are meaningful ways to carry your pet's love forward. Each action becomes a continuation of their life's impact, a testament to how they changed you.

Legacies are not about replacing what was lost; they're about expanding it. Every time you act from the love your pet gave you, their story continues. They live on in the wag of another dog's tail you help save, in the comfort you offer to another broken heart, and in the way you now see the world—with softer eyes and a more open heart.

Exercise:

Make a list of three Acts of Legacy that resonate with you. For example:

- Volunteer at a local shelter.

- Donate to an animal rescue in their name.

- Support a friend who is grieving.

- Create something beautiful—art, writing, or music—dedicated to them.

Once you've listed your ideas, choose one small act to complete this month. It doesn't have to be big or public—just heartfelt. Every loving action becomes a way of saying, "Your life mattered. Your love continues through me." In this way, your pet's legacy lives not only in memory but in movement—in every gentle thing you do from the love they left behind.

Acts of Legacy Brainstorming Guide

Activity

Love never disappears—it transforms. When you find ways to honor your pet through action, creativity, or kindness, you create a living legacy of their spirit. Every act of love, big or small, becomes part of the story you continue to tell together. "Legacy is not about what ends—it's about what continues."

Step 1: Reflect on Their Spirit

Before deciding how to honor your pet, spend a moment remembering who they were at their core.

What qualities or traits defined your pet's personality?

If your pet could leave a message for the world, what would it be?

How did they make your life or others' lives better?

Step 2: Brainstorm Legacy Ideas

Think of ways to express their memory through kindness, creativity, or contribution.

There is no single "right" way—only what feels true to your bond.

Type of Legacy Act Examples & Ideas Your Ideas

Acts of Kindness

Donate to a shelter, sponsor an adoption, send supplies to a rescue, pay for someone's vet bill

Acts of Nature

Plant a tree, create a garden stone, scatter wildflower seeds, volunteer for a park cleanup

Creative Acts

Write a poem, paint a portrait, make a scrapbook, record a tribute video

Ritual Acts

Light a candle each anniversary, hold a remembrance day, say their name in prayer

Sharing Acts

Tell their story online, join a pet loss group, educate others about compassion

Personal Growth Acts

Adopt again when ready, pursue animal care work, honor their lessons in your relationships

Which legacy ideas feel most meaningful to you right now?

Step 3: Choose One to Begin

Pick one act to start with—something simple, doable, and heartfelt.

This isn't about doing more; it's about doing what feels sacred.

My first act of legacy will be:

Why I chose this:

When I will begin:

Step 4: Legacy Tracker

Use this space to record your ongoing acts of remembrance and connection.

Date Act of Legacy Completed How It Made Me Feel

Which of these experiences brought me the most peace or joy?

Step 5: Reflection

What have I learned about love through creating this legacy?

How has this process changed my relationship with grief?

If my pet could see me honoring them in this way, what would they say?

Affirmation

"Your love lives through my actions. Every kind thing I do carries your spirit forward. This is our forever story."

My personal affirmation:

Legacy is the bridge between love and growth. Every step you take in their honor is a step toward healing—and toward spreading the love that they gave so freely. "You are gone from my sight, but never from my story."

The Blessing Ceremony
Guided Meditation

Welcome to The Blessing Ceremony.

This is a sacred moment to honor the love that continues — a bridge between memory and presence, between what was and what still lives within you. Find a peaceful space where you can be undisturbed for a few minutes. You might wish to place a photo, collar, or small token of your pet nearby. Light a candle, or simply sit in a soft, comforting light.

***

Close your eyes

Take a deep breath in through your nose... and slowly exhale through your mouth.

Let your shoulders drop.

Feel the weight of the day release from your body.

With every inhale, imagine drawing in peace.

With every exhale, imagine letting go of tension, guilt, or sorrow.

There is nothing to fix in this moment — only space to be.

***

Now, picture your pet in your mind's eye.

See them in their healthiest, happiest form — tail wagging, eyes bright, full of energy and love.

Imagine them surrounded by a radiant golden light — warm, gentle, and pure.

This light holds all the moments you shared: the laughter, the quiet companionship, the understanding that needed no words.

See them at peace — safe, joyful, and free.

***

Whisper softly, either aloud or in your heart:

"Thank you for loving me.

Thank you for teaching me.

Your spirit lives within me."

Take a moment to let those words echo.

You might feel warmth in your chest or a tingling in your hands — signs of love remembering its way home.

***

Now imagine the golden light that surrounds your pet beginning to expand — reaching toward you, shimmering gently as it moves closer.

As it touches your heart, it merges with your own inner light.

You and your pet's spirits intertwine — not in body, but in love, in memory, in soul.

Feel that light growing within you, filling your chest, your arms, your entire being.

You are not alone.

You have never been alone.

This bond, this love — it exists beyond form.

It becomes part of the energy that guides you, comforts you, and moves with you through life.

***

When you're ready, take one more deep breath.

Feel gratitude rise — for the time you shared, for the lessons learned, for the love that continues.

Blow out your candle slowly, watching the wisp of smoke curl and drift upward.

Know that the light of love has not gone out — it now lives within you.

Rest in this feeling of peace for a few moments longer.

Reflection Prompt:

What emotions surfaced during the Blessing Ceremony?

What sense of peace or connection remains within you now?

You may wish to journal about what you felt, or simply sit quietly, knowing that love — once given — never leaves.

The Light Lives On
Ritual

This final ritual honors the transformation of your grief into enduring love. It is a gentle acknowledgment that your bond did not end — it simply changed form. Through remembrance, gratitude, and continued love, your pet's light now lives within you, guiding how you give, how you care, and how you love others in their memory. This is not a goodbye. It is a continuation.

Create a Quiet Moment

Find a calm, comfortable place.

You may wish to sit by a window, in your favorite chair, or wherever you once spent peaceful moments with your pet.

Place a photo, collar, or another meaningful token before you.

Light a candle — a symbol of love made visible.

Connect to Their Memory

Take a few slow, deep breaths.

Feel your chest rise and fall.

Let your gaze rest softly on the flame.

With each inhale, imagine the warmth of your pet's love filling your body.

With each exhale, release the sadness that still lingers, allowing space for gratitude to take its place.

Speak Their Name Aloud

Whisper their name gently into the quiet.

Then say:

"Your love lives in me.

I carry it forward with gratitude.

You are forever part of my story,

and your light shines through my life eternally."

Feel the truth of those words resonate in your heart.

Love like this does not fade — it evolves, becoming the quiet strength that helps you show compassion, resilience, and tenderness in new ways.

Honor the Transformation

Watch the candle's flame flicker — steady and alive.

As you do, reflect on the ways your pet's love continues to influence who you are.

Perhaps they taught you patience, joy, or unconditional acceptance.

Let those lessons become your guiding light.

Close the Ritual

When you feel ready, take one final, deep breath.

Whisper a soft thank you — to your pet, to yourself, and to the shared journey of healing.

Then blow out the candle slowly, watching the smoke rise gently upward.

Imagine that light now glowing inside your chest — steady, peaceful, eternal.

The love you shared remains. It always will.

Reflection

In what ways does my pet's love continue to guide or shape me?

How can I honor their light through the way I live, love, and give?

Affirmation

"I am healing. I am grateful. I am forever connected to the love that began with my pet."

End-of-Chapter Self-Assessment Questions:

1. Do I feel more peaceful when thinking about my pet's memory?

2. Have I found a personal way to continue their legacy?

3. Do I feel stronger, softer, or more openhearted than when I began?

Chapter Seven

Chance's Legacy

This book was born from both my heart and my practice — from years of sitting beside grieving pet parents, and from walking through my own journey of anticipatory grief with my beloved dog, Chance.

Chance came into my life as a survivor — rescued from a puppy mill, shy but resilient, with a spirit that radiated forgiveness and trust. Over time, he became my shadow, my teacher, and the heartbeat of my home. He was there through new beginnings and endings, through laughter and tears, grounding me in a love that was pure and uncomplicated.

When Chance was diagnosed with hemangiosarcoma, I knew what the words meant — both clinically and emotionally. I knew the road ahead would require courage, presence, and acceptance. I began writing *Love Lives On* when Chance started chemotherapy. It became my way of walking road of anticipatory grief: one chapter, one breath, one act of love at a time.

Each page gave me a space to process the same truths I share with others — anticipatory grief is love preparing itself for change, that healing begins before goodbye, and that legacy is simply love in motion.

This book is his legacy. A promise that no bond formed through love is ever truly lost.

Thank you, Chance, for teaching me how to help others heal — by first learning how to heal myself.

At the time of Love Lives On's initial release Chance is doing well with his treatments, and we are grateful for each day post diagnosis we have with him.

Holding Space

Journal

The pages that follow are intentionally left blank. It's a quiet space for your heart to rest and create. Here, you can write your reflections, answer the prompts that resonated most, record memories, or simply let your thoughts wander.

You might fill these pages with photos, drawings, favorite quotes, or pawprints. There's no right or wrong way to use them — only what feels true to you. Grief and love both ask for expression. May these open pages become a place where your memories find form, and where your pet's spirit continues to live gently between the lines that aren't there.

www.ingramcontent.com/pod-product-compliance
Lightning Source LLC
Chambersburg PA
CBHW020459030426
42337CB00011B/156